Dr Pamela Douglas has worked in Australian general practice since 1987, with a special interest in women's health. She is the creator and ongoing developer of Neuroprotective Developmental Care or the Possums programs (www.drpam.au; www.ndcinstitute.com.au), which have been transforming new parents' lives since 2011, and is the author of over 30 international publications in the fields of crying baby, breastfeeding, and infant sleep research.

Dr Douglas is an Adjunct Associate Professor in the School of Nursing and Midwifery at Griffith University, and a Senior Lecturer in the Primary Care Clinical Unit at The University of Queensland.

She lives in Brisbane, Queensland, and has six adult children and stepchildren, and many grandchildren.

T0300805

THE
discontented
LITTLE
BABY
BOOK

DR PAMELA DOUGLAS

UQP

First published in 2014 by University of Queensland Press
PO Box 6042, St Lucia, Queensland 4067 Australia
Reprinted (revised and updated) 2018, 2019, 2020 (twice)

This edition published 2021
Reprinted 2021, 2022, 2023, 2024

University of Queensland Press (UQP) acknowledges the Traditional
Owners and their custodianship of the lands on which UQP operates.
We pay our respects to their Ancestors and their descendants, who
continue cultural and spiritual connections to Country. We recognise
their valuable contributions to Australian and global society.

www.uqp.com.au
reception@uqp.com.au
www.pameladouglas.com.au

A catalogue record for this book is available from
the National Library of Australia.

ISBN 978 0 7022 6545 7 (pbk)
ISBN 978 0 7022 6658 4 (epdf)
ISBN 978 0 7022 6659 1 (epub)
ISBN 978 0 7022 6660 7 (kindle)

Cover design by Christabella Designs
Cover photograph by Jade Brookbank / Getty Images
Author photograph by Andrew Porfyri
Typeset in 12/17 pt Bembo by Post Pre-press Group, Brisbane
Printed in Australia by McPherson's Printing Group

This book is not a substitute for medical advice and the publisher and the author
assume no liability. Please see your general practitioner if you have any concerns
about your own or your baby's health and well-being.

University of Queensland Press uses papers that are natural, renewable
and recyclable products made from wood grown in well-managed forests
and other controlled sources. The logging and manufacturing processes
conform to the environmental regulations of the country of origin.

For Elizabeth Grimes
who died in 1857 of puerperal mania
on Turrbal country

CONTENTS

NOTE TO THE READER

All the clinical cases I discuss in this book are fictional, although most of the situations I describe have arisen commonly, in many different permutations and various locations, over the years of my clinical practice. Any similarities to real people are completely coincidental. When referring to a baby, the pronouns 'he' and 'she' have been used interchangeably.

This book is not a substitute for medical advice. Please see your general practitioner if you have any concerns about your own or your baby's health and well-being.

PREFACE

Since *The Discontented Little Baby Book* first came out in 2014, scientists have laid bare the staggering dimensions of species extinction and climate crisis. And right now, women are giving birth in the midst of a devastating global pandemic.

The same social and market forces which drive us into catastrophic ecological breakdown shape the way our health systems care for parents with babies. Researchers tell us of the worldwide increase in medical over-diagnosis and over-treatment, including in babies. Instead of taking a 'complex systems' or 'whole ecosystem' approach to you and your baby's health and well-being, our health system and even our complementary therapists continue to create new diagnostic labels and quick fixes (which are regularly proven to be unhelpful in the long run). Researchers tell us that both health professionals and patients alike routinely overestimate the benefits of interventions and underestimate the possibility of side-effects.

The tendency to over-diagnose and over-treat unsettled baby behaviour, whether with pharmaceuticals, maternal diets, frenotomy, or even bodywork exercises, occurs at the same time as the most important underlying 'ecosystem disruptors' in breastfeeding and parent–baby sleep frequently remain unidentified.

In 2014, I wrote that eliminating foodstuffs from a breastfeeding woman's diet increased her baby's risk of allergy. This knowledge is now mainstreamed. Yet many babies who fuss at the breast are still inappropriately diagnosed with food allergies or intolerances. In 2014, I wrote that the infant gut microbiome plays a vital role in the development of the gut, immune and metabolic systems. This knowledge is now mainstreamed. Yet many babies who fuss are diagnosed with air swallowing and gut pain, which misunderstands the research. In 2014, I wrote of my concern about the diagnoses of posterior tongue-tie and upper lip-tie. Since then, the number of babies diagnosed with restricted connective tissues as the cause of their unsettled behaviour and breastfeeding difficulty has exploded, along with oral surgery and bodywork exercises, even though the evidence is clear that these diagnoses lack an anatomic or even functional basis. Subtle underlying biomechanical problems due to the way the baby fits into a woman's body during breastfeeding, so disruptive to her and her baby's capacity to feel in sync, continue to be overlooked. Sleep advice which makes baby sleep worse abounds. This health system confusion is historical, as discussed in Appendix 1, but perpetuated by a (gendered) failure to prioritise funding for primary care research into the clinical management of baby behaviour and breastfeeding problems.

One important change in the past seven years which I'd like to celebrate is that more and more health professionals are finding Neuroprotective Developmental Care (NDC or 'the Possums programs') effective for breastfeeding problems and unsettled baby behaviour. More and more parents are turning to the evolutionarily-aligned and holistic NDC programs for help (www.drpam.au; www.possumssleepprogram.com; www.ndcinstitute.com.au).

In these most uncertain of times, we are each called to do what we can for planetary health. Perhaps for you right now it's caring for your baby. Writing this updated edition of *The Discontented Little Baby Book* is my own way of doing what I can for the generations to come.

I wish you and your little one an abundance of joy!

Dr Pamela Douglas
Brisbane, 2021

INTRODUCTION

In the first days and weeks of new life, when you are still in a daze from the physical and hormonal tsunami of birth, something quite awful might happen. Your precious little baby may begin to cry for hours on end – shuddering screams convulsing that tiny, wondrous body, fists and limbs flailing, face red and screwed-up, little mouth open wide – and nothing you or anyone else does seems to help. Or it might be that your baby doesn't scream exactly, but just seems unhappy most of the time: grizzling, fussing and fretting, pulling away from the breast or bottle and waking frequently. In these situations, you might find yourself quickly overwhelmed by feelings of exhaustion and despair. Your partner or those close to you may feel helpless, too, as they offer what support they can.

One health professional might suggest that you space out the baby's feeds, watch for when she is tired, and put her down in the cot awake, with a view to helping her to 'self-settle'.

Another might diagnose gastro-oesophageal reflux disease, or allergy, or lactose problems, or tongue-tie, and prescribe treatment with medications, maternal diets, surgery, or bodywork exercises. Yet another might suggest that you 'breastfeed on demand', listen to your intuition, carry the baby a lot and avoid formula.

Whatever the advice, the underlying message can seem to be that you are somehow failing: if only you would stop being so weak-willed and sleep-train your baby; if only you eliminated the correct foods from your diet or carried the baby all day; if only you would show some guts and persist through your breastfeeding problems; if only you did the bodywork exercises often enough to stretch out and relax the baby's fascia; if only you were the intuitive type who had the capacity to work out what your baby wants.

Your friends might tell you that the fussiness relates to wonder weeks and developmental leaps – a comforting thought since neither you nor the baby are to blame. But you inquire into ages and stages only to discover that your baby fits none of them, since healthy babies mature in such different ways and at such different rates.

It's true that some babies are born with physical problems that require treatment, and some mothers do struggle with mental or physical illnesses that can interfere with the care they can give their babies. It's also true that the arrival of your baby will inevitably bring enormous change and adjustment, challenge and weariness, for you and your family, especially in the first 16 weeks. But a great deal of the tumult and misery of both woman and child in these first days, weeks and months can be avoided if they get the right kind of help and they get it early enough. Even when crying and fussing have set in, there is still a lot that can be done to make life easier for a family with a crying baby.

After nearly 35 years of clinical experience as a GP, including in my own mother–baby clinic, and 20 years of research in the field of unsettled infants, it's clear that the families of babies with cry-fuss problems can't be helped with a 'one-size-fits-all' approach, yet this is what most often happens. Health professionals obviously want the best for mothers and their babies, but tend to wear the lens of one particular discipline, whether it's behavioural psychology, medicine, lactation science, or bodywork therapy. There is often a lot of unnecessary pathologising. Cry-fuss problems need an interdisciplinary approach, integrating evidence from across many different fields including evolutionary biology and cross-cultural studies. This is why I have written *The Discontented Little Baby Book*.

Unfortunately, many parents are offered advice that arises out of a lack of trust in a baby's capacity to accurately communicate his basic biological needs, and also a lack of trust that responding to those needs makes life easier, not harder, for families. This breakdown in trust is quite understandable, for historical reasons. As a society, we've not been able to identify, let alone prevent, certain problems which interfere with the capacity of parents and their babies to get in sync. Life with a new baby often seems astonishingly chaotic and out of control as a result. Instead of learning to understand a baby's communications (or 'cues') in this situation, parents are advised to impose order in other ways. But the underlying problems remain unidentified, and lack of trust in the baby's cues can result in unnecessarily frequent night-waking, poor weight gain and low milk supply in breastfeeding babies and their mothers, in unsettled behaviours regardless of feeding method, and possibly even in an increased risk of obesity down the track for formula-fed infants. Most importantly of all, if parents are taught that they cannot trust their baby's cues, life with their little one simply isn't as pleasurable or as satisfying.

The Discontented Little Baby Book proposes a new way forward. It offers practical advice to help you identify and sort out problems that might underlie your baby's fussing and crying in the first months of life, regardless of whether you are feeding your baby breast milk or formula or both, and it encourages you to trust not only your baby's communications but your own ability to respond effectively (even if that seems impossible right now!). Chapter 1 explores why babies cry and how much crying is normal. Chapter 2 considers the unsettled baby's nervous system and why most babies have bouts of prolonged and unsoothable crying. Chapter 3 discusses the relationship between hunger pangs and crying, including why spacing out feeds can create problems. In Chapter 4, I explore the role of reflux and allergy in unsettled babies, and the effects of lactose overload in babies who are breastfed. Chapter 5 is all about feeding: how to get breastfeeds right from the very beginning, what mechanical and physiological problems might interfere, and how to bottle-feed in the healthiest way possible. Chapter 6 looks at the way babies are biologically hardwired to seek out sensory experiences and why settling practices such as placing babies in quiet rooms during the day can exacerbate crying problems and make life harder, not easier, for the family. Then, in Chapter 7, I examine the biology of parent–baby sleep and why it is often unnecessarily disrupted in our society. I discuss why we don't need to 'teach' babies to sleep, but only to remove the obstacles that get in the way. In particular, I consider why feed-play-sleep routines actually interfere with healthy baby-sleep. Finally, in Chapter 8, I offer strategies to help you manage the worried thoughts and feelings that inevitably arise when your little one is crying, fussing, and night-waking. These skills are drawn from a new wave of cognitive behavioural therapy that is sweeping the world of psychology and turning conventional approaches upside down.

My work is deeply embedded in the evidence, but there's no need to take everything I say as gospel – experiment for yourself. Families are resilient, and every family will work out what is right for their own unique baby and their own unique situation. By the time you've finished reading this book, I hope you'll have realised that *you* are your baby's best expert, that you will feel confident enough to try something different, and that you can trust yourself to find a way through until the crying and fussing and broken nights stop, as they will. It is also my hope that when the crying period is over, you'll find you've been practising a whole new set of psychological skills that will enrich the rest of your life.

I wish you many pleasurable hours with your baby!

1

HOW MUCH CRYING IS NORMAL?

Your newborn baby has not yet developed the capacity to speak to you using language. However, from birth she communicates her experience in a physical way: through the movement of her little limbs, through facial expressions, changes in skin colour and temperature, the way she turns her head, the sounds she makes, the changes in her breathing. We call her nonverbal communications her 'cues'. If she is experiencing something unpleasant, such as hunger, she is likely to begin telling us this with more subtle cues at first, such as grimacing and grunting, opening her mouth, moving her head from side to side in a rooting reflex or bobbing her head against your body. Then she may become increasingly agitated, with more jerky physical movement, small cries and grizzles, frowns, flushing, and back-arching. We might call these signs 'pre-cry cues', because soon they are likely to build into a full-blown cry if we are unable to work out what she needs or are unable to give it to her at that moment. A cry is a *late* cue. She's telling us that something is *really* wrong.

Of course, if your previously settled baby suddenly starts crying a lot, or has a temperature of 37.5 degrees Celsius or more, or vomits in a way that is different to his normal possetting, or if you have any other reason to think the baby might be unwell, it's important to see your doctor. Bouts of repeated or forceful vomiting after formula feeds, respiratory problems, or blood in the vomit or stool, for example, are signs that the crying baby needs to be medically assessed. However, less than 5 per cent of crying babies in the first few months of life have an underlying medical condition.

Mostly, unsettled babies are perfectly healthy. It's just that they cry and grizzle a lot, which happens to be heartbreaking for parents. Health professionals in the West have been saying for years that crying for prolonged periods is normal in the first 16 weeks, and won't hurt the baby. We definitely don't want families frantic with worry or lapsing into self-blame. We want to reassure them that the baby is healthy, and that this phase will pass without causing the baby any harm.

It's certainly true that most babies and their families are remarkably resilient, regardless of what happens, and will get through the crying period in the first few months without any long-term ill-effects. But when parents have such a strong feeling that their baby is signalling distress, our insistence that the crying is 'normal' can make it very difficult for them to trust in both their baby's communications and themselves.

If we consider problem crying in the first months of life across all cultures, we find that there are substantial differences between different societies. Babies *initiate* cries to communicate need or distress roughly the same number of times with a peak in the evening, no matter what culture they are born into, but they cry *for longer durations over a 24-hour period* in the West compared to traditional cultures. And interestingly, they cry for substantially longer periods in some Western societies, such as the United Kingdom, than in certain other Western societies, such as Denmark. Is it really normal, then, for a baby to cry a lot?

I think of 'normal' as a rhetorical device, a phrase that means, 'It's common in this part of the world; it's not your fault; it will pass without hurting the baby'. In this sense, crying in the first few months is normal. In 1962, Dr T Berry Brazelton described a 'normal crying curve' that had crying peaking at about 6 weeks. However, a recent meta-analysis of crying duration in twenty-four studies of Western babies demonstrates that they cry, on average, about 2 hours a day from birth until 6 weeks of age, before the crying tapers off to a little over an hour a day at 12 weeks, mostly disappearing by around 16 weeks (Figure 1).

Figure 1: Average amount of crying per day in Western babies

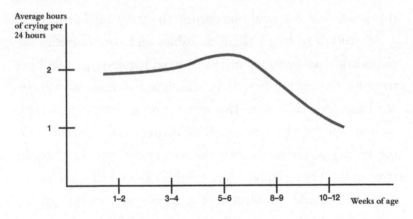

Adapted from Wolke, D. et al., 'Systematic review and meta-analysis: fussing and crying durations and prevalence of colic in infants', *The Journal of Pediatrics*, 2017; 185: 55–61.

So while crying a lot in the first 16 weeks is a normal phenomenon, this should never be confused with the belief that the baby's crying is not a communication of abject misery. Crying is a genuine appeal. Parents know this, in their bones.

SIGNS THAT OFTEN ACCOMPANY CRYING AND FUSSING

From both the medical literature and my years of experience in the clinic working with families and new babies, I've compiled a list of signs that often accompany a baby's crying and fussing:

- excessive feeding
- feeding refusal
- back-arching
- coughing, spluttering or gagging with feeds
- crying when put down
- vomiting
- frothy poo
- tight tummy
- copious belches and flatus
- very frequent waking
- won't 'self-settle'
- piercing shrieks.

Most parents will describe at least one or more of these signs in their unsettled baby, in addition to crying. They might tell me that their baby is unsettled, for example, because he wants to feed very frequently. He might pull away from the breast or bottle and back-arch. He might complain each time he is put down. He might posset or vomit a lot. He might have a lot of flatus or belching, a tight little tummy, and explosive frothy stools. He might seem to wake after only very short sleeps during the day. He might even be sleeping for only 30-minute or 1-hour periods during the night, a kind of excessive night-waking that happens sometimes in very little babies, in particular. Even though we know that, overall, an unsettled baby in the first few months tends not to wake up at nights more than others on average, he may not go back to sleep as easily, and night-time can be a nightmare of screaming, with everyone up and walking the floor.

KNOWING RISK FACTORS DOESN'T HELP

Research has linked many factors with excessive crying in babies (for example, being premature or small-for-gestational age; nicotine exposure during pregnancy; having a mother who experienced antenatal stress, a previous depression or birth complications; or having a father who was depressed during the pregnancy). That doesn't mean these factors *cause* crying in babies, and it certainly doesn't mean that you are *likely* to have a crying baby if you or the baby fall into these categories. In fact, this information is of little use to families, since it is rarely in a parent's power to change any of these factors retrospectively, and listing them makes everyone more worried and guilty. (Having said that, not smoking during pregnancy is important for a number of reasons.)

Some babies, due to inborn temperamental tendencies, might also be more susceptible to problem crying if things like feeding go wrong in the first hours, days and weeks. If everything had gone well at the beginning, that same baby may not have become a crier. Then, the baby's behaviour in the first weeks affects the parents' perceptions of the baby's temperament, which affects the way they interact with the baby, which affects the baby's temperament.

In the brand-new relationship between babies and their parents, problems can quickly interact in a downward spiral of distress. The reason why your precious little son or daughter cries a lot and shows one or more of the signs I have listed is often complicated, and might be unknowable. As we will see, 'quick-fix' solutions, from medications to sleep-training, while very tempting for us all, usually don't help, and sometimes make things worse.

We need to take the time to understand what lies behind these various signs and begin the detective work of decoding patterns, if we are to make sense of your baby's crying and arrest that downward spiral.

Jane: 'I feel like such a bad mother.'

Jane comes in to see me with her firstborn baby. He's 7 weeks old and is grizzling in the pram. She sits down and puts him in her lap. For a moment he looks around the room, but then his little face crumples and he begins to fret again, an incessant, upset, anxious sound.

'He wakes, oh, I don't know, half a dozen times from when we put him down for the night. It's really bad. I'm getting maybe

5 hours' sleep. And during the day he's either fussing like this or screaming, or sometimes sleeping, but he won't sleep for more than 20 minutes. When he starts to scream, there's nothing I can do.

'Oh, and he hates feeding,' she adds. 'At first he used to arch his back and pull off the breast, and wouldn't go back on even though I knew he was hungry. We started formula 2 weeks ago and he's been a bit more settled at night since then. The child health nurse has never been worried about his weight, but he still fights the bottle.'

'That must be hard for you,' I say.

Then suddenly, before I know it, she is in tears, shoulders heaving, wiping her eyes with the back of her one free hand and struggling to regain control. The baby arches his back on her lap and cries in earnest. She grabs three or four tissues from the box which is always ready on my desk.

'I feel like such a bad mother ...' she says with a sob.

'I can see you are an absolutely devoted mother!' I exclaim.

Jane confides through her tears, over the baby's racket, that she even feels ashamed to go out, for fear of attracting attention. For fear that others will think her incompetent because her baby cries.

Soon she is standing and jogging on the spot with the baby over her shoulder. He settles down a bit, and we converse to the sound of his grizzles. She tells me that her friend's baby girl lies in the cot cooing and gurgling before dropping quietly off to sleep. In fact, her friend's baby is happy to lie for an hour or two under a mobile gazing up at big red, yellow and blue felt flowers when her mother needs a break! She says her friend's baby only wants to feed every 3 or 4 hours, and sleeps through the night.

'But you see, babies' personalities are so different,' I explain, 'we just can't compare! Some babies *are* like your friend's little girl, although I have to say she's quite unusual. She's at the very far end of the spectrum of normal. Your little fellow is a high needs baby, that's for sure, right at the other end of the spectrum. Most babies lie somewhere in between, but they are all normal!'

Jane nods, jogging and patting.

Once I've finished asking the necessary questions, I check the baby over. He cries loudly as Jane undresses him then calms down a little, lying on the examination couch as we play with him and try to elicit a smile. He seems to be jumpy and easily startled, always on the edge of tears, with a subtle jerkiness to his movements. He's not easy to examine but I satisfy myself that he doesn't have a medical problem and is developing normally.

'Healthy babies are born with quite remarkable differences in their developmental maturity, too,' I explain. 'Boys are often much less developmentally mature at birth than girls. And the rates of development for different skills vary even for the same baby. One little girl might be quite late in being able to direct the movement of her hand, for example, but speaks words very early. She's still normal. Your little bubby is perfectly healthy, but you're right – he does cry a lot.'

Jane sighs in despair.

'We need to talk,' I say. 'I think there's probably quite a bit we can do to help settle him down. But did you happen to bring a bottle? Do you mind if I watch a feed first?'

2

THE CRYING BABY'S
NERVOUS SYSTEM

The human brain is extremely immature at birth and its neuronal pathways are the most 'plastic' or mouldable of any other baby animal. As a result, human babies are remarkably adaptable to a wide range of infant care practices across cultures. Tiny babies have been laced into cradleboards and swung from poles in the long house, or carried naked in polar bear fur against the mother's back through subarctic winters, or fed and carried in paperbark coolamons. They've had bindings and boards applied to elongate their little skulls. They've been transported down dangerous mountain tracks in billums, like plants. The different approaches to infant care across the kaleidoscope of human cultures have tended to have one thing in common though – until very recent times the baby has been kept close to the body of his various caregivers.

A woman's brain, too, is primed by the hormones of pregnancy and birth to be particularly plastic in the first weeks and months of her new baby's life. In this post-birth period, women look to the culture around them to determine how to be a good mother. In some cultures, good mothers burn dry wood and leaves in a pit in the ground and pass the baby through fragrant smoke. Or they put a knife under the baby's sleeping place, or bathe him in very cold water, or keep him inside the house to avoid the evil eye.

Because of their special neuroplasticity, mothers and babies are remarkably resilient in the face of the profound challenges of early life, experimenting together in their communications, constantly rebalancing, readjusting and finding synchrony as best they can in their own unique circumstances.

In a baby, the three fundamental biological processes of feeding, sleeping and sensory integration cannot be understood in isolation because they are profoundly interdependent, particularly in the first six months. The nervous systems and hormones of the mother/caregiver and baby interact to regulate these processes. (For example, the baby's suckling, or even just eye-contact and cuddles with the mother, causes the mother's brain to release the hormone oxytocin, which stimulates milk let-down, decreases her blood pressure and cortisol levels and floods her with feelings of relaxation and love.) These rewarding interactions between the caregiver's and the baby's nervous systems evolved throughout our long evolutionary history to maximise the survival of our infants and drive the propagation of the human race. Quite simply, when there is plenty of mutual pleasure, we can say that the parent and baby are 'in sync'. When a baby cries a lot, and there is a lot of distress for the parents, too, everything feels 'out of sync'.

THE MOULDABLE BABY BRAIN

From the first seconds, minutes and hours of life, a baby's brain is learning. (In fact, that amazing little brain was even learning in the womb!) By learning, I mean that the brain is laying down new neuronal pathways in response to experience. For example, after the birth a baby may learn to associate her mother's breast with warmth, safety and satiety of both milk and sensation. Similarly, it is not uncommon in the West, though no-one intends it, that a baby may learn to associate her mother's breast with distress and frustration because she has a feeding problem that no-one around her is trained to identify or to help with. This negative association is sometimes so powerful that it results in breast refusal, overriding the fundamental human drive for nourishment and survival. Formula-feeding, in this situation, may come as a great relief to both mother and baby, helping them get back in sync. In another common example, a baby may learn to associate the feeling of sleepiness with warmth, safety and satiety of both milk and sensation. She may also learn to associate being put down to sleep with an unpleasant sensory boredom, loneliness, misery or sometimes even a primal terror.

Once you understand the remarkable plasticity of the baby's brain, you will know that:

1. You and the baby are a remarkably resilient team, so even if you don't feel in sync you're both likely to get through the crying period without any long-term ill-effects.
2. You need to give yourself time to be flexible and experiment and get to know your baby if you are to bring your hormones and nervous systems in sync.

3. Getting help early on when you feel out of sync helps to ensure that problems aren't reinforced in the baby's neuronal circuitry and therefore harder to address.

A SENSITIVE FIRST 16 WEEKS

The tendency of human babies to cry a lot in the first 16 weeks marks this as a period of great neurological sensitivity. A phenomenal blooming of synaptic connections occurs in the brain during this period. Extraordinarily rapid brain development means, for example, that the newborn's brain uses up to 80 per cent of his metabolic energy at rest.

In the womb, many of the earliest nerve cells to appear in your baby's developing cerebral cortex are 'subplate' neurons. Subplate neurons act as a gateway in the wiring up of the grey matter. They receive pioneering sensory pathways, or axons, and then project their own new axons into specific areas in the cerebral cortex so that the wiring up of cortical circuitry occurs correctly. Subplate neurons also persist in abundance in the early months after birth, clustered together in what's known as the cortical subplate remnant, still helping to organise neuronal circuitry.

The subplate remnant intrigues me because its persistence is unique to the brain of the human newborn, which is so immature at birth. It is a distinguishing feature of a time when neurons are dramatically blooming and synapsing, when the brain is fabulously mouldable – and when babies are prone to crying. During this period, neuronal pathways are laid down in direct response to the stimulation that the baby receives

17

from his environment, becoming the templates for the rest of the child's brain development. The healthier and more diverse the sensory stimulation a baby receives in the first months after birth, the better the development of his brain circuitry.

As it happens, cry-fuss problems ease off at about the same time that most of the subplate remnant integrates into the maturing brain and disappears. This is also around the time a baby's nervous system and muscles are developed enough to move her limbs towards a goal; for example, to reach out with her hands for a toy. The abundance of the subplate neurons corresponds with a powerful biological need for healthy stimulation of the seven senses of touch, pressure, movement, hearing, vision, taste and smell, just when the baby is least able to procure any of this stimulation for herself. In the way I imagine it, the subplate remnant sits there in the baby's brand-new brain, a marker of unique vulnerability and immaturity amidst the great blooming of neuronal synapses, all of them ravenously hungry for the sensory experiences that will call forth the very best possible wiring up of the cerebral cortex.

It makes sense, then, that for many babies in the first 16 weeks, insufficient sensory stimulation is experienced as an absence, or a hunger, which makes them cry.

INCONSOLABLE CRYING

The amygdala is an almond-like structure buried deep in the baby's brain, hardwired for the swift identification of danger, either in the environment or in the body. Once the amygdala has registered some kind of threat, internally or in the baby's environment, it activates the fight-or-flight response, which involves the sympathetic nervous system and hypothalamic-pituitary-adrenal axis.

With low levels of sympathetic nervous system activation, the baby signals for help with little grimaces, or grizzles, or slightly agitated movements. She might start rooting (turning her head from side to side) or bobbing her head against her mother's body, looking for the breast if she's hungry for milk or for the sensory stimulation of a feed. If the discomfort or threat continues, the amygdala continues signalling and the fight-or-flight response builds. When the sympathetic nervous system is turned on full bore, the stress hormones adrenaline and cortisol course through the baby's blood vessels, causing flushing, sweating, pounding of the heart, quickened breath, perhaps a rush of blood to the limbs – and screams. It may be difficult to know exactly what triggers your baby's crying but you can be sure that her amygdala has detected something that is worrying or uncomfortable. The amygdala's reactivity is affected by the baby's temperament and individual level of maturity at birth.

Luckily for all of us, we also have the parasympathetic nervous system, known as the 'rest-and-digest' part of the involuntary nervous system, to counterbalance or dampen down the fight-or-flight response. The rest-and-digest response turns on when a good filling meal reaches our gut (or when we take a deep breath in, hold it, and then let it out again). Filling up your baby's tummy not only turns on the parasympathetic nervous system, the associated touches and cuddles and loving eye-contact trigger the release of oxytocin in her brain, to make her even more relaxed and sleepy.

Once a baby is worked up and crying hard, it can be really hard to settle her. This is because the nervous system activity of the fight-or-flight response itself triggers more of the fight-or-flight response, in a powerful feedback loop. It might be that all you can do then is to wait until the crying bout has run its course, and fatigue overwhelms her nervous system. It helps to understand that this is what's going on, though, and that it's not your fault if she won't settle once the crying is underway. For some babies, a difficult-to-soothe crying bout may occur a number of times a day, last anywhere from 40 minutes to a couple of hours or more, and is often worse in the late afternoon and evening.

The tiniest thing can set them off

The way I see it, infants who have repeatedly frustrating experiences, such as unidentified feeding problems, may not only have long periods of fussing or bouts of inconsolable crying (i.e. repeated lengthy bursts of high intensity sympathetic nervous system activity), but may also develop a temporarily sensitised amygdala and hypothalamic-pituitary-adrenal axis. It's as if the thermostat on their stress response has been reset to a lower threshold. They begin to cry at the drop of a hat. They react to tiny, difficult-to-identify triggers as if they are huge problems, wake with a piercing shriek, seem nervous and jerky in their movements, and fret, cry and scream day after day, even once the initial triggers are no longer relevant. For example, a baby with an unidentified feeding problem in the first days and weeks might continue to behave as if he is very highly strung throughout the rest of the crying period, with frequent crying bouts, even once the family, in despair, change to formula.

The good news is that this neurological sensitivity usually settles down by about 16 weeks, as the baby's brain circuitry matures and the cortical subplate disappears.

THE GUT IS A 'SECOND BRAIN'

In a baby, the gut is a soft and glistening muscular tube, 3 metres long and a centimetre or so wide at birth, suspended from filmy membranes threaded with blood vessels and lymph and nerves, and coiled up in the abdomen. Waves of contractions pulse through it, propelling milk from the back of the mouth down through the oesophagus, stomach, small intestine, large intestine and rectum to the anus, where it squirts out as a sweet, digested, mustardy liquid. The gut has a hundred million nerve cells embedded in it. These belong to the enteric nervous system, the third part of our involuntary nervous system. The enteric nervous system connects to the brain through the sympathetic nervous system, the parasympathetic nervous system, in particular the vagus nerve, and by chemical and hormonal messengers. For this reason, the gut is a feeling organ, very sensitive to brain changes, and is often referred to as 'the second brain'.

When the sympathetic nervous system is turned up high, particularly for long periods, the gut changes. Muscle contractions of the oesophagus, stomach and intestines alter, causing more reflux or vomiting or delayed emptying of food from the stomach. (In adults, for example, depending on the individual's constitution, stress can cause diarrhoea or constipation and, in situations of extreme stress, vomiting.) If the sympathetic nervous system is constantly on red alert, this can affect the composition of the gut microbiome and makes the gut wall more permeable, affecting the immune system. However, the composition of the milk a baby drinks is the most powerful cause of change in gut microbiome – that is, formula changes the bacteria of the gut away from the protective evolutionary ideal, with flow-on effects for the immune system since it is so intimately connected with the gut. That's why even a small amount of breast milk is protective, if you can do it.

COMMUNICATING WITH YOUR BABY

There is a great deal of neurological and psychological research to show that babies develop best when there is good two-way communication between the baby and his parents and other caregivers. I refer to this good two-way communication as 'cued care'.

We've already talked about how your baby communicates her experiences to you through her physical and behavioural cues. When you are offering cued care, you are trying to respond to her cues as best you can so that her fight-or-flight response is activated as little as possible, and her rest-and-digest response is activated as much as possible. This is how you both stay relaxed and enjoy each other.

Right now, this might seem to be a ridiculously unobtainable goal! But even if it's not possible to stop your baby crying, doing your best to communicate with him and help him in the midst of all the confusion and crying is deeply protective. In the following chapters, you will see that there are many potential obstacles to synchrony between the nervous system and hormones of mother and baby that are not a parent's fault, and which have effects that may be difficult to remove or change during the first sensitive 16 weeks (though we can certainly try). In particular, I'm talking here about the effects of birth complications and unidentified feeding problems. However, once we've done what we can to minimise obstacles, you dramatically increase your chances of feeling in sync with your baby if you practise cued care. Cued care between parent and baby is rather like learning to dance together. It takes a great deal of practice at first to get the steps right – often you are out of time with each other, there are lots of spills and bumps, but then you right yourselves again and move forward, until it gradually starts to feel easier.

Why cued care is so important

One day soon no-one will talk about 'cued care' at all: we will simply talk about looking after the baby, or about getting in sync with the baby as best we can. But right now I need to use the term 'cued care' to differentiate it from some very popular recommendations. I expect you've heard of them. New parents are regularly advised to either *not* respond to their baby's cues, *delay* their responses to their baby's cues, or respond in a way that is *different* to what they know is the baby's intention when he gives a cue. (I talk more about these recommendations in later chapters.)

Cued care doesn't mean we have to respond immediately to our baby's every communication. This is impossible anyway, especially when our baby has older siblings who also need our attention. It also doesn't mean we should expect our baby to be completely relaxed and happy all of the time. Cued care simply means we offer a pattern of sensible responsiveness to our baby over time – *an intention to respond*, not *an intention to delay*.

Recommendations to delay responses to your baby's communications have the aim of teaching him to 'self-settle' at night, and also, very often, to space out feeds. In fact, 'self-settling' has become something of a holy grail in the first year of new families' lives. A baby who is said to self-settle doesn't need parental assistance to get back to sleep if he wakes in the night, or at least learns to sleep for longer periods without disturbing his parents. Parents are told that the strategies for teaching the baby to self-settle are evidence-based, and best for their baby's development.

Unfortunately, the evidence shows that this approach not only doesn't help families, but can make things worse, resulting in more crying and fussing and less sleep for everyone. If things aren't going well, families are told to apply the strategies for self-settling even more rigorously. When these strategies don't work, parents begin to feel they must be failing.

When you are told to deliberately delay responding to your baby's cries; when you are told to ignore the powerful biological cue of sleepiness at the end of feeds many times a day; when you are given a list of infant communications and are told to interpret them as 'tired cues', rather than experimenting with the meaning of your baby's communications for yourself, it's no wonder that the whole business of trying to understand your baby's communications, and to communicate back effectively, becomes extremely fraught.

3

HUNGER PANGS

Could some babies cry a lot because they are hungry?

This is a controversial thing to suggest in the cornucopia of the West, where fresh produce crams our fridges, where pantries overflow with packets and jars, where a decision to dine out means choosing between fine cuisines from many different countries. My claim that many babies cry in the West because they are hungry may make some health professionals, who are as protective of mothers and babies as I am, really quite angry. None of us want parents thinking that they are starving that new little person, who is their own flesh and blood! Nor do we want to put our babies at risk of obesity later on. So I'll ask you to be patient with me while I explain.

In many respects, to parent *is* to feed in the early weeks and months. Yet for historical reasons (discussed in Appendix 1), our society has a gaping blind spot about infant feeding and this is why most health professionals still sincerely believe it's not possible that some babies are crying because of hunger!

Indeed, our training in this area is so poor that many of us have no idea how to identify feeds gone awry – or we actually give advice that might *cause* feeding problems (such as spacing out feeds, introducing 'feed-play-sleep' cycles, or limiting time at each breast). The baby's crying is metabolically expensive, too, using up calories at a great rate. This means long bouts of crying actually create a catch-22 situation: the infant is too upset to feed but needs *more* feeds.

Indeed, a well-conducted study shows that crying babies have lower levels of the hormone cholecystokinin in their blood after feeds. Cholecystokinin is known, amongst other things, as the hormone of satiety, released when a high-calorie feed fills the stomach and passes into the small intestine; the cholecystokinin then travels in the blood to the brain, where it signals satiety, or satisfaction. This finding of lower cholecystokinin levels supports the claim that some babies cry a lot because they're hungry.

The newborn experiences hunger as extremely stressful – a life-or-death matter – which makes sense in evolutionary terms. When things go wrong with feeds, babies panic. They are hardwired to signal hunger with a great deal of distress. As we saw in the previous chapter, if a feeding problem is not detected early enough, some babies' nervous systems become sensitised and they might continue to cry a lot throughout the sensitive first 16 weeks, even once their biological needs for satiety are better met.

IS MY BABY GAINING ENOUGH WEIGHT?

This is a question that worries many mothers, who rely on health professionals to guide them. Worldwide, we have conventionally taken 100–120 grams a week to be an adequate baseline weight gain for newborns and young babies. A baby gaining weight like that is definitely not starving! But in 2006, the World Health Organization published growth charts that demonstrate the rates at which large numbers of breastfeeding babies grow across multiple countries in optimal circumstances. These show us that healthy breastfed babies gain, on average, 200–255 grams a week in the first two months of life. That is *twice* the 100–120 grams a week we have considered to be an adequate baseline weight gain! Many happy breastfed babies gain 300 grams, or occasionally even 500 grams in a week at this age. Mothers often worry that those chubby rolls of fat, those wonderful little 'Michelin tyres', put the baby at risk of obesity later on, but this kind of weight gain in breastfed babies doesn't increase your child's risk of obesity, and is more likely to protect against it. Dramatic weight gain in breastfed babies in the first few months of life is biologically normal.

As parents we can't look to numbers to tell us what our baby needs: instead, we pay attention to the baby's communications and trust that by responding to her cues we will meet her requirements. And some babies, who are gaining weight adequately and definitely not starving, cry a lot because they need more calories.

WHY PARENTS USE FORMULA

You'd think our breasts would know what to do. All on their own during pregnancy, breasts become more vascular and more glandular – hotter and tighter, bigger and heavier.

You'd think that the ancient mammalian part of a woman and her baby's brain would know how to breastfeed.

The truth is, we *can* trust the body's competence, we can rely on a profound bodily intelligence in both mother and baby during breastfeeding – as long as obstacles haven't been put in the way at the very beginning, as long as the people around a mother and her newborn *know how to help them get in sync*. But if the care that a woman receives from the health system is unable to prevent, or accidentally creates, breast pain for the mother and distress for the baby; if health professionals are not trained to identify and repair problems that arise in an affordable and timely way, what are a new mother's options?

In Australia, almost all women want to feed their newborn babies from their own body alone, but by the end of the first week, one in five are using at least some formula. By the end of the crying period, more than half of Australian babies receive another food, usually formula, for at least part, if not all, of their diet. The research tells us that mothers report three main reasons for beginning formula:

1. The baby is crying and fretting.
2. The baby isn't growing adequately.
3. The mother has excruciating breast pain.

It's not because women fail to appreciate the benefits of breast milk, or because they lack willpower. It's because, for many mothers and their babies, breastfeeding just doesn't work. And if things are going wrong with the getting of milk, babies cry, because the craving for milk is the craving to survive.

Even when breastfeeding more or less works, for some women it remains difficult, exhausting and stressful – to be endured. The baby pulls off, frets, grizzles, screams, bites, back-arches, feeds incessantly and barely sleeps. The breasts hurt a lot, whether from mastitis or nipple abrasions. When, despite the great courage of a woman's efforts, the baby is weighed and she is told he isn't gaining properly, she may be devastated and wonder if breastfeeding is worth the distress.

This is why some health professionals regularly advise mothers to space out and limit feeds – they care deeply about women's distress, and they still believe that constraining breastfeeds must surely minimise breastfeeding's potential disruptions to a woman's health and well-being. In the West, given our history, the pragmatists' belief that breastfeeding is tough, and needs to be carefully regulated, makes perfect sense.

When breastfeeding advocates claim that almost all adult human females can breastfeed, they are right, too. In an environment where women have grown up observing easy and successful breastfeeding all about them, and have internalised the body-memory of feeding patterns and positions; when birth has occurred without medical intervention, so that the mother's hormones and the baby's primitive feeding reflexes aren't muddled; when new mothers are surrounded by experienced women with intergenerational expertise in the support of breastfeeding – in that world, almost all women can breastfeed their baby. But in our real world today, we often don't see women breastfeeding until we've had a baby of our own, caesarean sections and other interventions might delay the milk coming in or interfere with primitive neonatal reflexes, and the rising prevalence of chronic diseases poses extra challenges to lactation.

Human babies are hardwired from the first moments of birth to locate the breast and reach out with their mouths for milk. Today, it is health professionals who are responsible for setting up an environment in which the baby can demonstrate this competence after birth. Often, once we've set up the right environment at the beginning, helping babies take their mother's breast is not so much about what we do, as about what we don't do. It's about getting out of the way.

And it's health professionals who are responsible for identifying and helping with any problems that arise as early as possible in the following days and weeks. Yet as we've seen for historical reasons most aren't trained to either prevent certain breastfeeding problems or to identify them, and even unknowingly give advice that makes things worse. This historical blind spot would also explain why a number of studies show that breastfed babies cry more than formula-fed babies. I don't mean to be disrespectful to all those dedicated health professionals who give everything they have in the support of women with new babies; it's just that I think we have to be real about what is in fact a societal problem, shared by all of us. Too many mothers blame themselves.

Kate: 'I can't take this anymore.
I'm starting some formula.'

Kate has had an implant for a hypoplastic left breast, which did not develop in adolescence, and comes to see me with her partner and their 6-week-old baby. Despite the hypoplastic breast, she is determined to breastfeed. She's even built up some milk on the left. We plot out weights, and the baby is gaining an average of 120 grams each week, but never seems satiated.

'She's either feeding or crying,' Kate says, shaking her cropped dark hair, 'and she only ever has short sleeps.' The baby is at her breast while we speak and I notice the fit and hold is good.

'At nights,' Kate continues, 'she seems to wake every hour or even more. During the day, she only sleeps for 10 minutes or half an hour at the most, and she cries whenever I'm not feeding her.'

Kate is pale, with dark circles under her eyes from the sleepless nights. She is reserved, careful and determined, sitting there calmly in jeans with her black T-shirt pulled up to feed.

I ask, 'How many heavy wet nappies a day do you think?'

The baby's father is taciturn and a little defensive, protective of his partner's commitment to breastfeeding. She sighs and shoots a weary glance at him. He takes over and begins to answer my questions with the confidence of a man on active duty.

'Probably six,' he says.

'Good,' I say. (Disposable nappies are so absorbent that it can be hard to tell how many wet nappies the baby has had. Mostly, it's important that the urine is clear or only pale yellow – not concentrated and strong. But five or six heavy, wet disposable nappies in 24 hours is a good urine output.)

'And stool? The baby's poo?' I ask.

He shrugs. 'Three or four times a day; probably more.'

This baby is definitely not starving. A spread of liquid stool in the nappy perhaps the size of a palm a few times a day is good stool output. Kate's heroic efforts mean that this baby is receiving enough milk – just – and has good output. But the 'marathon' feeding and constant waking tell me that she is often hungry.

Frequent feeding is normal early on, and can feel quite overwhelming in the first two or three weeks, while the baby is getting used to sucking and learning to be more efficient. But this family's situation is severe. This is not the usual exhaustion of the first few weeks, when the baby feeds every couple of hours or sometimes in clusters that seem to run together, but often drops off the breast milk-drunk, sleeping happily for a time, with plenty of periods of alert calm eye-contact and pleasurable interaction. Kate's story, of the unsettled marathon feeder, is typical of underlying feeding problems which result in poor transfer of milk from breast to baby. In Kate's case, her breast tissue on the left is not producing milk as easily as it should, and since many babies will feed perfectly well from just one breast, it is possible her right breast has been somewhat affected too. Certainly her baby is never satiated.

'You're doing great,' her partner says quietly to Kate, and she smiles wanly. He turns to me. 'I'm so proud of her,' he says.

'Yes, she's amazing,' I reply. 'She really is.'

He nods. We watch Kate and the baby for a moment: suck-suck-suck-suck-suck-suck-suck-suck-swallow-suck-suck-suck-suck-suck-suck-pause.

I can tell from this baby's pattern of sucking that the milk transfer is poor, at least in the feed I'm watching. Even though she is gaining weight adequately, it's at a substantial cost to Kate – the long hours feeding, the extremely frequent waking, the baby's fussing and crying – a price Kate has been willing to pay, so far.

There's no easy solution. Kate's already been doing everything possible to help build her supply in both the good and the hypoplastic breast: switching from breast to breast two or three times in the one feed, feeding to cue, pumping after feeds.

I talk with Kate about her values. She is deeply committed to breastfeeding.

'Can you clarify for me why that is?' I inquire gently.

'I want that closeness,' she says after a while. 'It's definitely best for her, and really, I just want that closeness.'

'So you value providing your baby with physical closeness, and you want the best for your baby's health?'

She nods.

'This is one of those very tough situations where despite doing all the right things, even with adequate weight gain, she's just not satiated. That's why she's feeding all the time and crying so much,' I say.

Tears are falling down Kate's cheeks. She looks steadily down at the baby, suck-suck-suck-suck-suck-suck-suck-suck-pause.

'Only you can decide when you've had enough. She's gaining just enough weight, so you could continue on as you are. But I suspect that's not sustainable,' I say. Kate shakes her head briefly.

'It's not,' her partner says.

Then I add carefully, 'It would be possible, it seems to me, to hold to your values, even if you are not solely breastfeeding.' Her partner reaches over and touches Kate's hand, there against their cherished baby's back for a moment, and her tears fall silently onto the little girl's forehead as she feeds with concentrated attention.

I run through the options. 'You could continue on as you are, and we'll just monitor the baby's weight, or you could introduce formula in a bottle two or three times a day, so that the baby is able to be satiated. Some women in your situation like to look for donor milk.'

She says quietly, still looking down, 'The lactation consultant suggested a supply line.' (That's a thin little plastic tube that runs from a container with milk along the breast to the nipple.)

The baby's father sighs with some frustration, clearly not convinced.

I say, 'Yes, that's an option too. It would make sure your breasts had as much stimulation as possible.'

Then Kate looks up, suddenly determined. 'I'm not doing a supply line,' she says firmly, wiping away her tears with the back of her hand. 'I can't take this anymore. It's not good for her, either. I'm starting some formula.'

4

TUMMY TROUBLES

'Her little tummy was upset last night but she's settled down now,' parents say of their baby's crying. They have reason to believe that their little one's tummy is a site of unpredictable and sometimes violent events, which result in pain and screaming. But is this really the case?

'Colic' was originally a medical term for spasm in a hollow organ. From at least the mid-18th century it has also been used to refer to cramps in the intestines of babies, causing crying, purportedly due to wind or constipation or vague 'gut upset'. Considering the spicy paps and gruels upper-class babies were fed, I'm sure that many did suffer a true intestinal colic! Then, in 1954, Dr Morris Wessell defined a 'colicky' baby as one who cried for 3 hours a day, on 3 days a week, for 3 weeks or more. That was 60 years ago, when most Western women didn't breastfeed, and available breast-milk substitutes were often quite unsafe for brand-new little intestines.

The term 'colic' is outdated now. The gut *is* still involved in cry-fuss problems, but not always in the way people think. And the term 'colic' arbitrarily labels the upper end of the spectrum of crying and fussing as a medical condition of some sort, which isn't helpful. It doesn't matter how long a baby cries and fusses for each day: if parents are concerned about the crying then it needs to be taken seriously, even if we can't necessarily stop it.

DO MEDICINES OR COMPLEMENTARY THERAPIES HELP?

It's tempting to try out various remedies that are advertised or popularly recommended for the treatment of baby 'colic', in the hope of some relief. Many parents, in desperation, buy Simethicone over the counter at their local pharmacy for their crying baby. The manufacturers claim that Simethicone (or Infacol) relieves 'colic' by helping small gas bubbles in the baby's stomach or intestines join into larger gas bubbles, which are then more easily passed. Not surprisingly, since gas in the gut is really only a cause of crying in breastfed babies who have a lactose overload, treatment with Infacol has no more effect on parents' reports of crying than a placebo. The prescription medication Dicyclomine sedates the baby and is not safe to use in this age group because of the risk of breathing difficulties and seizures. Many people think that homeopathic remedies must be safe because of the very low concentrations of active ingredients, but homeopathic remedies prescribed for crying babies have been linked with toxic effects. Various other complementary and alternative therapies including acupuncture and herbal or 'gripe water' formulations show no benefit when researched.

IS IT REFLUX?

The first thing to note as we embark upon the controversial topic of gastro-oesophageal reflux disease (often referred to as GORD, for short) is that milk reflux is more or less pH neutral, certainly not particularly acidic, for the first couple of hours after a feed. The acid in any stomach content (that is, in any 'reflux') that runs up into the oesophagus and even spills out of the baby's mouth is thoroughly buffered by milk, whether breast milk or formula.

Once, the professor who edited a medical journal disputed this in a paper I'd submitted. He cited a couple of studies, and I had to point out that those studies were performed on older infants who had not fed for more than 2 hours. I directed him to other studies on babies in the first few months of life and he conceded my point. The acidity and toxicity of reflux over time depends on how often babies are fed, and with what. Fruit juice, for instance, is highly acidic when it refluxes (and nowadays we recognise that it is not suitable for babies!).

When a doctor puts an endoscope down the oesophagus of a baby who fusses and pukes a lot, it is very unusual to see patches of inflammation, known as oesophagitis or GORD. In fact, we try to avoid endoscopy in babies, because anaesthesia brings its own risks. (I should mention, however, that oesophagitis does occur more often in babies with underlying problems such as neurological abnormalities or a floppy windpipe.) The oesophagus is pristine at birth, and it takes frequent, repeated bathing in acidic fluids over a period of time for inflammation to develop. Perhaps oesophagitis was more common in this age group decades ago when babies were expected to go for prolonged periods between feeds, so that they regularly refluxed undiluted gastric acid, or when they were routinely fed juices and solids and wheat-based products and cow's milk mixtures from the first weeks of life.

It also takes a long period of severe allergic response to cause damaged tissue in the lower oesophagus, and again, it would be extremely rare to see this in the crying period. Sometimes, when we take a biopsy of the baby's oesophagus and put it under the microscope, the pathologist might see some allergic white cells in it. But there is simply no reason to believe that these cells, in the absence of visible inflammation, cause pain that results in feeding problems and screaming babies.

Many parents of crying babies are still told to hold the baby upright after feeds, or to raise the cot or pram at the head-end or sleep the baby on wedges, yet elevation obviously doesn't help if the reflux isn't harmful. Even if there's been a long time between feeds and the reflux is acidic, it can only hurt if there are already inflamed or ulcerated spots in the lower oesophagus, which is almost never the case. Imaging studies show that there is no basis to the diagnosis of Aerophagia Induced Reflux, or the idea that some babies swallow very large amounts of air with feeds resulting in reflux and pain. Every now and then you might also hear it said that the baby must be screaming due to the sensation of the oesophagus stretching. I'm afraid this strikes me as a last-ditch attempt to hold onto the oesophageal pain explanation, given that the many other reasons babies cry are neglected!

Some doctors like to distinguish between 'vomits', involving powerful stomach contractions, and 'spills', when the milk seems to slide back up and out effortlessly, but this distinction isn't helpful either. If you are worried that your baby has consistent projectile vomits, or looks sick and pale after feeds, see your doctor to rule out any serious underlying condition such as pyloric stenosis or food protein-induced enteropathy syndrome. However, the force of reflux depends on various factors, including pressure on the abdomen and the effects of a fight-or-flight response. Normal healthy babies vomit frequently, with varying force, including some projectile vomits. In fact, research shows that two-thirds of babies vomit regularly, and that the vomiting peaks at 4 months of age.

Some doctors also diagnose 'silent' reflux in crying babies, said to run up the oesophagus and cause pain, without running out of the mouth in a spill or vomit. But the fact is that everyone has 'silent' reflux. All of us, babies and adults, reflux regularly – it's just that the fluid is more likely to rise right up and out of a baby's short little oesophagus. In adults, the reflux will often be quite acidic, due to the foods we eat and the spaces between meals, but even then that won't hurt us (unless it happens so often and is so acidic that we have already developed patches of inflammation). Rarely, babies can have reflux-related respiratory problems, but again, these don't cause oesophageal pain or cry-fuss problems.

Julia: 'But he pukes all the time!'

Julia's 9-week-old firstborn, with his shock of red hair, screams for long periods especially in the afternoons and evenings. She breastfeeds him four times during the day, and also when he wakes at night, which could be as often as three times between 10 p.m. and 6 a.m. He vomits half a dozen or more times a day, especially after feeds. The paediatrician diagnosed reflux 2 weeks ago, and commenced him on Losec.

'It's already made a difference,' Julia says. 'His pain and vomiting haven't completely settled but they've eased off a bit.'

I listen quietly. The evidence clearly shows that these medications have the same effect on parents' perceptions as placebo – but the placebo effect is very powerful, resulting in a 40 per cent or 50 per cent improvement in the amount of crying parents report. Also, Julia's baby will now be on a trajectory of decreased crying, regardless, as the sensitive period passes.

'I came in because I wanted to know if I should increase the dose.'

She points out her baby's restless, grizzly behaviour in the pram, saying that he fed just half an hour ago and that his reflux must be playing up. Then he spills, a milky fluid pulsing out from his mouth.

'See what I mean!' Julia exclaims. She opens her nappy bag and finds a washer to wipe his face and the dark blue fabric of the pram.

To my mind, this is the grizzle of a bored baby wanting a much more interesting sensory experience than the one he is getting, lying flat on his back in a closed-in pram in a closed-in consulting room.

I take a careful history, examine the baby (which settles him because he loves the interaction!) and we talk for a while.

'Do you think he has reflux?' she asks, looking me straight in the eye.

'Well, by definition he has reflux,' I reply slowly, 'because that's what a puke or vomit is. As to whether he has gastro-oesophageal reflux disease – inflammation in his lower oesophagus that makes him cry—' I hesitate. I prefer not to contradict another doctor's diagnosis and will usually send a patient back to their doctor to discuss any concerns they have. But when a patient directly asks for a second opinion, I do my best to be honest. I take a deep breath.

'The reflux that runs back up the oesophagus (and sometimes out of a baby's mouth) is not particularly acidic within 2 hours of a feed. The pH is closer to neutral, whether the baby has been fed breast milk or formula.'

Julia looks startled.

'So why do we have to keep the baby upright for half an hour after feeds to stop the reflux? Why do I have to use the wedge at nights? I thought it was to stop the acid coming back up.'

'I agree it doesn't make sense to try to elevate babies: the reflux running back up from the stomach isn't acidic enough to do any damage for a couple of hours after feeds. The milk dilutes and buffers the gastric juices.'

'But he pukes all the time, before or after he cries,' she says. 'He seems to cry as if it's hurting. I've been told he's swallowing air with his feeds.' She rummages around in her nappy bag again and produces a notebook in which she has diarised the vomits. They occur more frequently after feeds, and may be projectile. 'I never go anywhere without bibs and towels,' she continues, uncertainly. 'I'd really like your opinion.'

I regard her for a moment, shift in my chair to get comfortable, and begin carefully. 'We do have to make sure there's nothing nasty happening, but both the paediatrician and myself have done that, and in my opinion there's no other problem. I know from the research he won't be swallowing air when he breastfeeds. And two-thirds of babies vomit regularly. It's completely normal and slows down after they're about 4 months of age. This is just how he is!' The baby gazes at me, transfixed, from his mother's lap. He's much happier now that he can see the action.

'Mind you, what you say about the big vomits after feeds makes sense, because a baby is more likely to vomit if the tummy is very stretched. I'm still not worried about his possetting, but he'd possibly cry less if you fed him more frequently. That's something you could experiment with if you wanted.'

Julia looks at me anxiously. 'My friend's baby is only 2 weeks older, and cries even more than mine. It's really bad, and they had the monitoring done, and the doctor said it was definitely reflux.'

'That sounds awful. Of course it's hard for me to comment on your friend's baby because I don't know the ins and outs of their case. But what I can say is that monitoring doesn't help us make a diagnosis of inflammation in the oesophagus. Monitoring just tells us how acidic the fluid is and how often it refluxes. But all sorts of things influence that – how often the baby is feeding, whether the baby is crying, how the baby is positioned.'

I can see this is hard for Julia to believe when she's heard something different from so many other respected doctors. It's been estimated that there's something like a 17-year gap before what we know from the research becomes usual practice.

'They said that their baby's reflux was so bad, he couldn't

gain weight! Apparently he coughed and gagged and arched his back and vomited whenever they tried to feed him.'

'It sounds like a nightmare,' I say.

I think to myself how rare it is that vomiting babies fail to gain weight due to the vomiting itself. The coughing, gagging, back-arching and refusal to feed, so commonly attributed to gastro-oesophageal reflux disease, are most often due to underlying fit and hold problems, or sometimes a conditioned dialling up at the breast, and it's the unidentified feeding problem that causes the poor weight gain.

I turn my attention back to Julia's little boy.

'If a baby is feeding well, we don't need to worry about the milk that is lost in the vomits – the baby easily compensates for that,' I explain. 'But maybe we could focus on late afternoons and evenings, when he cries the most?'

'Lots of babies cry at that time of day, don't they?' she asks, stroking her baby's downy red hair as he locks his gaze on her face.

'Yes that's true,' I reply. I begin to inquire further. I learn that Julia loves to cook (or she used to, anyway, before the baby was born). She'd always imagined that one of the bonuses of being on maternity leave would be having more time at home to get creative with food. She's usually in the kitchen with the baby in his pram from late afternoon. Although she picks him up for cuddles quite often, he screams and screams without responding no matter what she does. It's very stressful, in fact sometimes she feels quite angry, so she puts him back in the pram and tries to calm herself by preparing the meal.

'Have you ever tried to breastfeed him more often at that time of day?' I ask tentatively. He's gaining weight just fine, at

150 grams per week, but it's clear to me that this baby needs to breastfeed more often, especially at the end of the day, if he is to be more settled.

'I used to, and it did stop him crying, but he vomited a lot and I could never get anything done. I was told I should space out the feeds to every 3 hours, for his sake, because I was over-feeding him which caused the reflux.'

Once I explain that many babies need to feed frequently at that time of day, and that they can't be overfed at the breast, Julia starts to feel hopeful. I suggest she comes back in if she thinks it might help for me to observe a feed, but the only feeding problem that seems to emerge from her story is the problem of feed spacing.

I am impressed by how flexible Julia's thinking is: soon she is planning how she could both enjoy preparing the evening meal *and* feed the baby more. She decides to prepare parts of the dinner earlier in the day, when it's easier. She will invest in a slow cooker. She decides to buy a good quality baby carrier, since she enjoys being in the kitchen so much. This will free her up to do at least some of the food preparation with the baby enjoying the sensory stimulation of swinging around the kitchen with her. When it is time for the less safe aspects of her cooking, such as chopping or time at the stove, she'll try positioning the baby in the pram so he can see her.

When she wheels the pram into my room a fortnight later, Julia tells me the evenings aren't perfect, but she's enjoying them a whole lot more. Not only can she take pleasure in cooking again, with her little boy gazing out from the carrier or pram, tummy full, but also his father now takes him out for walks some evenings before they eat. Previously, her husband hadn't felt confident to do that because of the crying. They've stopped worrying about the vomiting, too. And she saw the paediatrician to begin weaning her son off Losec.

'It does take twice as long to get anything done,' she laughs, 'but it's definitely worth it, to have him happier!'

When a diagnosis makes things worse

The story that gastro-oesophageal reflux disease (GORD) causes crying in the first few months may not be accurate, but it has given families something to hang on to. 'Reflux' has become code for 'screaming baby, parental misery' and reassures mothers and fathers that the crying is not their fault. At a time when no-one had much else to offer, this diagnosis kept parents sane.

However, an inaccurate diagnosis of GORD in the crying period may not only perpetuate the family's distress because underlying problems remain unidentified, but may also create illness down the track. This occurs because fussy, vomiting babies are commonly treated with proton pump inhibitors and other medications that suppress acid production, even though the studies show they are no more helpful than placebos. Acid-suppressing medications not only increase the risk of serious infections, they increase the risk of bone fracture in later childhood. And they increase the risk of allergy or asthma.

How does the increased risk of allergy happen? The large food proteins which transfer from a mother's diet into her breast milk are less likely to be digested when the secretion of gastric acid is suppressed, although as we have seen, the stomach is not terribly acidic in the 2 hours after a feed. Importantly though, anti-secretory medications make the gut wall leaky. This means that large undigested food proteins can cross over into the baby's bloodstream and cause an allergic response.

When a baby is screaming a lot, three things happen that affect the gut:

1. There are long spaces between feeds (because the baby is in a crying feedback loop and can't feed), which means any reflux is more likely to be acidic.
2. The baby's sympathetic nervous system is turned up very high, which means that reflux will occur more often due to altered intestinal contractions.
3. There is raised abdominal pressure (from the baby's tummy muscles tightening during screams), which also causes reflux to occur more often.

As a result, it is far more likely that lots of crying and fretting eventually causes oesophagitis as childhood progresses, than it is that oesophagitis causes crying in the first months of life!

A'nh: 'It was GORD all along.'

A'nh arrives for her regular pap smear in a fitted black sleeveless dress and heels. She works as the CEO of a large nonprofit organisation, just down the road, and it's her lunch break. She slips off her shoes, stockings and knickers behind the curtain, and lies patiently on the couch covered by a sheet while I tear the sterile packaging off the slide and brush and speculum. She mentions she has a son in primary school and I ask about him as I prepare. The story pours out.

'We had a very bad start,' she says. 'He screamed nonstop

for the first 4 months.'

She explains that at night he would sleep for about 40 minutes, wake up screaming and take an hour or more to breastfeed. During the day, he still took an hour or more to feed, and slept only if A'nh carried him. However, he gained weight adequately and was developmentally on target, so the professionals A'nh saw in those early weeks told her that her baby's unsettled behaviour was normal.

'I'm still angry about that,' she says.

When her baby was 4 months old, and still exclusively breastfed, the local child health nurse found he wasn't gaining enough weight. A'nh was referred to a paediatrician, who diagnosed gastro-oesophageal reflux disease and prescribed Losec.

'The specialist said that when they have silent reflux, they go to the breast then pull off in a certain way due to the pain.' She demonstrates for me, extending her spine on the couch and turning her head to the right, and then to the left, just as the paediatrician had shown her, just as her baby did at the breast. The paediatrician also advised her to introduce rice cereal, and to hold baby upright for 20 minutes after feeds.

At last, things improved. A'nh's baby still only slept in his cot for 20-minute blocks during the day but at least he slept for around 2 hours at night before wanting a feed, and the feeds were shorter. It still took ages to get back to sleep, since it was hard to settle the baby after holding him upright after feeds.

'So I don't have very good memories,' she says, as I finish up. 'Now we know it was GORD all along, and it took nearly 5 months to get a diagnosis.' I nod quietly, spraying fixative onto the slide of the sample I'd taken.

'I think it took me a long time to bond with him as a result.'

'I'm not surprised,' I say. 'That's a really tough beginning.'

'But everything's fine now, luckily. He's a beautiful boy.'

As she dresses behind the curtain and gathers her things to leave, I think of how many times I've heard versions of this story over the years. At first, A'nh and her baby had been managing to compensate for poor milk transfer, caused by an unidentified feeding problem, with long and frequent feeds. Pulling off and back-arching at the breast signal a feeding problem, often of fit and hold. The baby screamed from poor satiety, and had severely interrupted sleep due to hunger, or the disruptions of having to burp and hold upright after feeds. As his calorie needs increased with maturity, A'nh's heroic efforts weren't enough and the baby failed to thrive. It's not surprising that the situation quickly turned around with the introduction of solids.

A'nh has been told that the GORD must have been there all along, undiagnosed, and that it caused her baby to cry from the very beginning. It's true that the early months with her son *were* marred by a serious undiagnosed problem, just not the kind that she thinks. All I can do is to admire her courage.

IS IT ALLERGY?

The only food allergy or intolerance that might have any association at all with crying in babies is to cow's milk, and even then cow's milk allergy or cow's milk protein intolerance tends to be over-diagnosed. Its incidence is actually low in early life. Eliminating dairy products from a breastfeeding mother's diet for 2 weeks is enough to determine if there is a difference in the baby's behaviour, but I usually only suggest this strategy once we've worked through everything else that is discussed in this book.

It makes sense that formula puts a baby at increased risk of cow's milk allergy, because formula is a concentrated dose of cow's milk protein placed directly into the baby's gut many times a day. Even then, cow's milk allergy in babies most commonly causes skin rashes and constipation and occasionally blood in the stool – not crying.

For many years, pregnant and breastfeeding women were advised to eliminate all sorts of food proteins from their diets in the belief that this would protect their children from allergy, especially if they had any hint of allergy or intolerance themselves. They were also told to do this to help stop their babies crying. This latter advice relied on the findings of one prominent Australian study – though the findings of that study could be explained by cow's milk allergy alone.

It is now believed that maternal elimination diets actually *increase* a baby's risk of allergy down the track. Exposure in the first 6 months of life to the small amounts of food proteins found in breast milk helps stimulate a baby's immune *tolerance*. A healthy, protective gut microbiome is important in the development of this immune tolerance. Allergy appears to be triggered, in the situations we are discussing, either by the gut effects of proton pump inhibitors, or by exposure to a food protein in the absence of built-up tolerance.

Affected families know how disruptive and frightening true food allergies in their children can be. In Australia the prevalence of paediatric food allergies is higher than anywhere else in the world. Many possible causes have been canvassed, including over-sanitation, antibiotic use, and environmental toxins and pollutants. But the diagnoses of gastro-oesophageal reflux disease and food allergies in crying babies in the first 3 or 4 months began here in Australia, and became very popular at home before spreading internationally. In fact, the diagnosis of GORD in crying babies first arose in my home city of Brisbane when I was a young doctor, and I watched it spread like wildfire through the southern states and overseas, while real and treatable causes of crying behaviours, such as feeding problems or an unbalanced sensory diet, were overlooked.

The gut is the largest immune organ in the body, and very immature in the first weeks and months of life. The gut microbiome is protected by breast milk, but sensitive to disruption. As we've seen, treatments for the diagnoses of GORD and food allergy directly and powerfully affect the baby's gut, either through the medication she is given or, if she is breastfed, through her mother's elimination diet. These two popular treatments for cry-fuss problems therefore have a direct and daily impact upon the development of the immune system – a far more direct effect, I'd argue, than household cleaning products, a short course of antibiotics, or environmental toxins.

A familiar pattern emerges: the baby who cries a lot (whether due to an unidentified feeding problem or hunger for more sensory nutrition or due to something else less knowable) is misdiagnosed with a medical condition. The baby is put on acid suppression medications, predisposing to allergy. Or the mother is put on an elimination diet, predisposing the baby to allergy. Allergy emerges as the baby grows older, which is assumed to retrospectively explain the problem crying.

But if we take away our explanatory diagnoses, what's left?

Medical diagnoses have been important because they have helped protect women from the belief that the baby's crying must be their fault. I think this is why the diagnoses have been so attractive to doctors: we've been anxious to protect women from thinking they are 'bad mothers', which is so clearly not the case. Also, of course, as professionals we don't want the families who come to us to go away empty-handed or feeling unsupported – we want to give them something to hold on to.

This is why in my research over the past 20 years, I have integrated the evidence from across many different fields to challenge conventional medical thinking about crying babies, developing a new and more holistic way of offering families the help they need.

Tanya: 'When the breast milk hits her stomach, she's immediately in pain.'

Tanya's baby is 3 months old and has been very unsettled right from the beginning. The baby vomits frequently after and in between feeds, and during feeds often pulls off the breast and arches her back, fretting and refusing to go back on. Yet she seems to be gaining weight adequately.

Tanya saw a lactation consultant three times in the first 2 months, when she'd had some nasty nipple damage, but that resolved. Towards the end of that time, the baby had blood streaks in her vomit, so Tanya went to see a paediatrician and then a paediatric gastroenterologist. After performing an endoscopy, which didn't show any gastro-oesophageal reflux disease or other problem, her doctors told her that a food protein allergy could be causing the unsettled behaviour.

By the time she comes in to see me, Tanya is no longer eating soy, eggs, wheat, nuts and dairy products. She is at her wit's end. She doesn't feel she can keep breastfeeding, because of the allergies which make the baby so unsettled, and because it is so difficult eliminating all these foods from her own diet.

'How did your doctors say the allergies were affecting her?' I ask. (Often the whole suite of signs which can accompany crying and fussy are attributed to allergy.)

'In the tummy, I guess,' Tanya replies, vaguely. 'The blood in the vomit. The green poo.'

I think to myself that the blood streaks in the vomit were most likely to be due to the baby swallowing blood from the nipple damage and then refluxing it in the milk. In any case, the endoscopy was clear, confirming the bleeding wasn't from oesophageal inflammation. When I inquire, I discover that her baby's stools are quite normal for a breastfed baby. Mucousy, green poo is common, and not a cause for worry, unless the baby is sick with a true gastroenteritis. Although blood in the stool should always be discussed with a doctor, even that doesn't necessarily signal allergy or serious pathology. I quickly abandon this line of questioning. There is something else going on.

'You can tell how sensitive she is when the breast milk hits her stomach,' Tanya adds. 'She's immediately in pain.'

'Oh dear,' I say. 'Can I watch a feed?'

It is heartbreaking. Tanya sits on the edge of the comfy lounge-chair in my consulting room, holding her breast awkwardly with one hand, elbow winging outwards (she is understandably nervous because not only is the whole experience incredibly stressful but now someone is watching), and the baby swings up over the nipple and attempts to come on briefly. Then she fusses and frets and pulls off, back-arching, turning her head this way and that. She latches on and sucks desperately for a few minutes, her little head and neck somewhat tucked under to try to get onto the breast. Soon she pulls off, quite unable to achieve a stable feeding position the way Tanya is holding her, and Tanya's nipple falls to point to the baby's chin, another sign of poor positioning. Before we know it, the baby is crying loudly.

'See?' Tanya says over the cries, despairingly. She stands up, puts the baby on her shoulder, and begins to pat. 'It's often like this. Other times she'll stay on for a bit longer before the pain gets to her.'

I do my best to help Tanya, who has been utterly heroic in her attempts to make breastfeeding work. I grab the doll and knitted breast I have on hand for demonstrations and suggest that perhaps she could try a different way of holding the baby when she feeds. I demonstrate the steps of the gestalt approach, explaining as sensitively as I can, but she really can't hear what I'm trying to say. I see in her eyes that my suggestions seem ridiculous to her. I'm wagging a doll around talking about *how to hold the baby*? When all the other doctors have diagnosed pain in the gut from an allergy – a serious medical condition? How could something as simple as the way she holds her baby *begin* to explain the hell she's been through? She tells me again she's about to give breastfeeding up, anyway, and after my suggestions are quietly rebuffed, I realise that changing to formula might be a sensible way forward for the whole family.

A week later, the baby is weaned and taking an extensively hydrolysed formula (hydrolysed means the cow's milk proteins have been broken down by enzymes into much smaller parts).

The baby's behaviour improves dramatically. Tanya and her other doctors attribute this to the effects of a low-allergen formula. Certainly the evidence shows that crying babies who are already formula-fed are more settled if they change to extensively hydrolysed formula, which would suggest they have a true cow's milk allergy – although I only recommend a formula change once we've tried everything else.

In Tanya's case, however, I know that her baby settles down only because the horrible distress of trying to breastfeed with so much breast tissue drag is over: at last, the baby is satiated.

IS IT LACTOSE OVERLOAD?

Sometimes, a breastfed baby cries a lot because of lactose overload. This is the only situation in which we need to worry that the baby might be experiencing true gut or wind pain. When a baby has lactose overload, her mother typically has a very generous milk supply. Although the baby may be stacking on weight, there is still no reason to worry about overfeeding. Nor is there anything wrong with the milk or the baby's gut enzymes. The baby's gut microbiome is likely to be altered – but it's the lactose-related fermentation and gas which cause discomfort or pain, not the accompanying dysbiosis. This baby can be helped, often with dramatic improvements within a few days, if breastfeeds are managed differently for a time.

Lactose is the most important carbohydrate in human milk. It is dense with energy and provides 40 per cent of a baby's caloric needs. Lactose has a proportionately stable concentration throughout a feed: the more milk your baby swallows, the more lactose travels into his gut. Needless to say, when you notice a suck-swallow-suck-swallow-suck-swallow pattern, the baby is drinking down higher volumes of milk and higher loads of lactose. When you notice a suck-suck-suck-suck-suck-suck-suck-swallow pattern, he is drinking less milk and less lactose is going in.

The breast is constantly secreting all components of the milk, including fat globules (which I'll call cream). Unlike lactose, the cream content in breast milk is variable, gradually increasing over a feed as the volume of the milk and the amount of lactose decrease. If baby is feeding flexibly and frequently, and going back to the same breast in a short period of time, then the milk in the next feed contains less lactose, due to the smaller volume.

The lactase enzyme in your baby's small intestine breaks lactose down into glucose and galactose. These molecules are vital sources of energy and are rapidly absorbed. However, if he receives very high loads of lactose over time, the capacity of the lactase to break it down may be exceeded. Undigested lactose draws water into the gut lumen and causes increased intestinal contractions. Usually very little undigested lactose gets as far as the baby's colon, but when there is lactose overload, lots of undigested lactose arrives in the colon and is fermented by bacteria. Gases, lactic acid, and short-chain fatty acids are released. This is when a baby might:

- develop a bloated tummy
- have acidic, frothy, explosive, frequent stools
- pass lots of wind
- cry a lot.

If this continues over time, the baby may also:

- never seem satisfied but want to feed and feed from the breast
- gain weight very rapidly.

Lactose overload is a spectrum condition. Often a baby might have a touch of it in the first weeks if you have a generous supply, but nothing much needs to be done. Your breasts will often be full, which inhibits milk production, and your supply gradually decreases to better match the baby's need. Some women find things go best offering just one breast a feed, at least for a time. But it's only occasionally that lactose overload causes serious fermentation in the baby's colon, requiring changes in how breastfeeding is managed. We need to be careful: we definitely don't want to cause a woman's supply to drop off so much that her baby now cries a lot because he's not receiving enough milk!

Although babies with lactose overload have normal amounts of the lactase enzyme, some doctors still prescribe lactase drops, despite research showing lactase drops don't help. The problem has been called 'hyperlactation' by the Americans; in Australia we call it 'functional lactose overload'. It's really just a result of receiving too much lactose with feeds over a period of days, caused by breastfeeding challenges like very high supply or switching sides more often than the baby needs. Imagine, though, the irritation to the lining of the colon (not to mention the changed bacterial populations) if this acidic fermentation is happening, day in and day out! No wonder these babies cry.

Sometimes, a gastroenteritis or true cow's milk allergy causes temporary damage to the gut lining, affecting the production of lactase. If the baby is formula-fed, a formula that is free of lactose, or of both lactose and cow's milk protein, may be called for. If the baby is breastfed, breastfeeding should continue, though a maternal cow's milk elimination diet may help while recovering – but this kind of lactose problem is not linked to cry-fuss problems.

Toni: 'Talk about poo explosions!'

Toni's 4-week-old baby cries for 4 or more hours a day, and for long periods during the night. He fusses and back-arches during feeds. He screams at the end of a feed or whenever Toni tries to put him down. He vomits a lot, too, especially after feeds. He has copious flatulence, explosive frothy liquid stools five or six times daily, and at least the same number of heavy wet nappies. He sleeps for 20 minutes at a time during the day, and Toni is lucky to have hour-long blocks of sleep at night. He either shares his parents' bed so that she can snatch a little more rest, or sleeps in a bassinet beside them.

The baby is gaining weight marvellously well, over 300 grams a week. In fact, one health professional told her just a few days ago that she was over-feeding him and that Toni should space out the feeds to every 3 hours.

'If he's not sleeping, he's crying,' Toni tells me, in a controlled voice that quavers at times, betraying the enormity of her exhaustion and despair. 'I feed him because it's the only thing that shuts him up.' She looks at me with a determined and courageous expression and brushes her carefully blow-waved fringe out of her eyes.

'I got through it with the first two,' she says. 'I breastfed them both and I'm determined to do the same with this one. But I'd like to make sure I've tried everything.'

She tells me that her paediatrician has already prescribed Losec, because of the baby's symptoms and the family history. Her first two babies were diagnosed with reflux from the first days of their lives – each one screaming for the first 6 months, during which time she breastfed them exclusively.

'This is an extraordinary story,' I say. 'How remarkable that you breastfed your children in the face of all that stress!'

Both her elder son and her daughter were on proton pump inhibitors for much of their first year, and weaned at 12 months. Neither of them slept through the night until they were about two, and the eldest now has a number of allergies and attention deficit hyperactivity disorder; the second has a cow's milk allergy.

'I used a carrier with them both until it became like an appendage,' she says. 'But I don't want to repeat the same mistakes. I set up such bad habits with the older ones – they never learned to self-settle! I want to do it differently this time.'

As we talk, the baby is dozing restlessly or wriggling and grizzling and passing wind in his pram. Consultations with new families are always punctuated by various little gut events, mothers diving for a cloth to wipe away spills, loud burps, red baby faces puckered in concentration, the unmistakeable sound of a nappy filling. But Toni's baby is spectacular: our consultation is distinguished by the sheer quantity and volume of those background baby-farts!

When I watch a feed, Toni's baby suckles easily, but soon pulls off with a fabulous splutter and spray of milk. And then follows an uneasy feeding session, with lots of pulling off, the milk spraying and dribbling, the baby fretting, desperately bobbing and panting, back-arching and making little cries.

'He's been a fussy feeder from birth, like my other two. I'm so envious of women who sit there with their babies calmly feeding. I never feed in public.'

'I think there are two problems,' I say quietly. 'One is that you have such an abundant supply of milk.'

'Oh, God! I could feed triplets. Quadruplets,' she exclaims. 'It sprays out everywhere – he can't cope with it.'

'Well, I think he is fussing so much in good part because I can see he's not quite positionally stable. Usually, particularly as they grow out of the newborn stage, they cope with vigorous let-downs as long as they are fitting into the breast well. We could look at that later. But the other challenge is your wonderfully generous supply.' The baby suddenly splutters and pulls off, as Toni has another let-down. Usually after the first one in a feed, women aren't aware of their let-downs, but Toni always knows because the baby pulls off, choking and dribbling. We hear a loud gurgly stool.

'Talk about poo explosions!' she says, inspecting his nappy. 'It's unbelievable.' The baby is making agitated little cries. 'Often it runs out of the nappy and all over him!'

'Yes,' I say. 'When the baby repeatedly receives high loads of lactose, which happens a lot with a generous supply, the capacity of the lactase enzyme to break it all down in the small intestine is exceeded. Undigested lactose reaches the colon, where it ferments to create all that gas. That's why he has such a bloated tummy, and explosive poos, and so much crying.'

Toni is staring at me, astonished. Suddenly, she gets it.

'That's it! This is exactly what's happened with each of my babies! Oh my God ...'

Toni continues to shake her head, putting the baby back up on her shoulder and patting him. 'You poor little bubby,' she says, and her eyes fill with tears. 'This makes so much sense! I can't believe that no-one has picked it up all these years! I just can't believe it!'

A number of different breastfeeding problems have the end result of lactose fermenting in the baby's colon. In Toni's case, it is her magnificent supply of milk, enough to feed multiples. This is the problem that has made life miserable and stressed and exhausted with her three precious little children, day after day, week after week, month after month, conceivably setting the eldest, at least, off on a trajectory of a sensitised stress response into later childhood. The treatment with proton pump inhibitors may also have predisposed them to allergy.

So what can I offer?

'It's still important to feel you can offer the breast frequently and flexibly. The baby may pull off very quickly because he's taken what he wants and is ready for another sensory adventure. The key here is to return the baby to the same side over a period of time,' I explain to Toni. 'We want to let the other breast run full in order to dial down it's milk production. But there are no fixed rules. Just experiment.'

'Oh,' she says, 'I've always fed from both breasts each feed ...'

'Yes, for most women we suggest feeding from one breast until the baby has finished, and then offering the other side. At the beginning, the milk usually needs to be removed from both breasts each feed, and often, to establish supply. But once a mother understands the principles, she can experiment and sort out what works for her own unique breasts if it becomes obvious the baby has lactose overload.'

'Should I take him off when I get a let-down and let the milk run?' she asks. 'So he gets less?'

'That's a strategy. We wouldn't have you pump milk off because that would stimulate the supply. I think the best plan is to gradually decrease your supply by letting both breasts run as full as possible, without triggering mastitis. That is, watch out for comfort, and don't let them overfill. But the less they are emptied the less milk they will generate. Feeding from one side over a few hours, then the other side for a few hours, does that. It's very much trial and error, to suit your individual breasts and baby.'

In a situation like this, the strategy of spacing out the feeds might seem to help because it effectively suppresses the milk supply. The problem is that for many other mothers and babies, this one-size-fits-all strategy fails to identify underlying problems, undermines milk supply, and can make crying worse, due to hunger.

Toni and I meet weekly for a time, until her youngest is more settled. Her supply remains rather high despite our best efforts, although the baby's positional instability is much improved after we've worked together. She also finds he needs much less time on the breast than she previously thought. He still cries more than she'd like, but not nearly as much as he was, and he's sleeping better. At least his tummy is no longer upset.

'I can't believe that a baby can be this easy,' Toni reflects during our last meeting, before I hand her care back to her usual GP. Then she laughs. 'Okay, I'm exaggerating. It's still damn hard work, with the three of them. What I mean is that he's not screaming all the time. I can put him down in the pram or on the floor and he'll lie quite happily on his own for 5 or 10 minutes. He even drops off to sleep sometimes at the breast!'

WHAT IS THE ROLE OF GUT BACTERIA?

New studies show that the composition of bacteria in the gut of babies who cry a lot is different from those who don't, right from the first few weeks of life. There are increased counts of *Escherichia Coli* and decreased counts of the protective *Bifidobacterium* and *Lactobacillus* in a crying baby's gut microbiome. It's being said in some quarters that this altered bacterial profile must indicate a gut cause, after all, for babies' distress, but this is too simplistic. There are many ways in which the gut, the brain, the immune system, and gut bacteria all interact and influence each other. To give you one example, high levels of sympathetic nervous system arousal alter the composition of gut bacteria over time and also increase gut permeability, affecting the immune system in ways that are only just being explained.

There has been a great deal of interest in the use of probiotics, or friendly bacteria, in crying babies, in particular *Lactobacillus reuteri*. Studies show that this specific strain, administered in drop form, decreases crying times in breastfed babies (if they've been crying excessively). It's worth trying for a few weeks, although many of the babies who come to see me are already on it – and they still cry and fuss a lot! Probiotics don't help, or may even worsen, crying in formula-fed babies.

Inflammatory markers are elevated in crying babies, both in the stool and in the bloodstream. But it's interesting to me that the crying baby studies which investigate the role of gut microbiome, probiotics, and markers of inflammation fail to take into account the interactions between the gut as 'the second brain', gut microbiome, stress, and clinical breastfeeding problems. This oversight reflects our historical blind spot concerning breastfeeding. The fermented products of a lactose overload, for example, would be expected to increase inflammatory markers in the stool. A crying baby, with her chronically dialled-up sympathetic nervous system, would be expected to be in a (temporary) pro-inflammatory state. It seems likely to me that breastfed crying babies responded to probiotic drops because the probiotic offsets the effects of lactose fermentation for some. However, the appropriate (and far more effective) treatment would be management of the underlying breastfeeding problem. We can't really know what role *Lactobacillus reuteri*, inflammatory markers and gut bacteria might play until we have research that controls for the treatable clinical breastfeeding problems which affect the gut in crying babies.

5

FOR THE LOVE OF MILK

In this chapter I want to consider how to prevent or help resolve the early breastfeeding problems which so often trigger crying and fussing. If you've already weaned your baby, you'll find the sections at the end useful, because in the sensitive first 16 weeks, formula-feeding is also best offered in response to your baby's communications, using the strategy of 'paced' bottle-feeds rather than according to the clock.

THE FIRST BREASTFEEDS

At birth your baby, like any little mammal, is a bundle of twenty or so hardwired feeding reflexes. These reflexes are directed with the singular force of millions of years of evolutionary history towards bringing the mouth onto the breast and suckling. If your newborn is placed freshly born on your bare belly or chest, touch, scent and visual cues activate these reflexes. The pressure of soft flesh ledges on her feet cause her little legs to pull up and push down, crawling forwards. She bounces her face against you, hands opening and closing. The sight of your breast, a looming mound of flesh and nipple, and the chemical scent of your areola, call her. Once she is there, her little hands may pat your breast, orienting her. If her mouth finds her own hand this, too, only helps orient her, and in time she'll move it out of the way. If she swings her head to and fro, urgently, she is looking for the feeling of your breast against her cheeks and face: when she feels the pressure of the breast against her cheek, she will turn her face towards it. She might sniff and lick the nipple.

It's important to resist the temptation to move the breast in to help as she comes on. Eventually she orients enough to bring her mouth over the nipple, just where it falls, and to bury her face into your breast. The baby's upper back and neck are surprisingly strong as long as she has a stable position against your body, her belly and chest flat against you, pulled in against you by gravity. It helps to hug her to you with a hand across her upper back between her shoulder blades, so that she can bury the lower half of her face in deeply.

A baby doesn't need to take more breast from under the nipple than from above, or be lined up in a nipple-to-nose orientation. We don't have to be watching her tongue, or trying to make her gape wide in order to latch on deeply. Her mouth simply presses in, her face makes a seal, and she begins to suckle. She will soon draw up a good mouthful of breast as well as nipple and areola between the enfolding warm bed of the tongue and her hard palate. Before long, the tip of the nipple rests near the junction of the hard and soft palate, a surprisingly long way back in the mouth. The jaw and tongue draw down in a deep instinctual rhythm, creating a vacuum and rhythmic pressure changes to extract the colostrum.

Having the baby in skin-to-skin contact (that is, just in a nappy against your bare chest if you are the father, or between your breasts if you are the mother) settles newborns. Mothers and babies need lashings of unhurried skin-to-skin contact and many practice runs over the first hours and days after birth to lay down the neuronal circuitries for breastfeeding. These practice runs may not even end in feeds, and that's fine. You don't have to rush your baby. His stomach at birth is only the size of a cherry, and doesn't expect much milk for a few days, until your milk comes in. Luckily, since you might still be recovering from the birth, you don't have to do anything much other than lie back a bit, get comfortable, and make your body available. It's the body contact that counts, offering plenty of opportunities for his reflexes to kick in when he's ready. The colostrum is a few precious drops of antibodies, a liquid gold which lines and protects his little gut and therefore his immune system like magic paint, a few millilitres of it extracted with each of the first feeds.

Babies quickly build on the first feeding experience by experimenting. When you notice your newborn looks even slightly upset, perhaps bobbing her head or shaking it, grimacing and panting as if she is trying to find the breast, lean back a little on the chair or bed, and bring her skin-to-skin between your breasts. If you place her upon your warm skin, upon the sound of your breath and your voice and your beating heart, her feeding reflexes are triggered and she will move to your breasts, bobbing and twisting. Responding to even mildly upset cues, particularly when the baby is very young, with a breastfeed as soon as possible keeps her fight-or-flight response turned down and her rest-and-digest response turned up. She learns best when she is in a calm, alert state.

At first, breastfeeding often feels awkward and clumsy. It helps if you are as relaxed as you can be. Imagine that you are sinking down into the chair or bed. Consciously release any muscle tightness that you notice, taking several deep breaths, releasing tension with each exhalation. You need to be positioned so that your arms, shoulders and neck are well-aligned (that is, not at odd angles), so that you don't develop musculoskeletal pain. Your muscles shouldn't have to work holding the baby: gravity does that. He needs to be lying horizontally across your partly reclined body, his belly and hips and chest flat against you, his pelvis and legs tucked up under your other breast, or wrapped around the opposite side of your body to the breast he is feeding from. Pillows under the baby often get in the way of good fit and are best avoided.

You are on a journey of physical learning together, attending to your body's sensations, attending to her little communications and wriggles. Let your body's sensations and her communications be your guide. Nestle her in and slowly move her, millimetre by millimetre, until she fits without discomfort or pain. In the gestalt method we refer to these tiny experimental movements that you make as 'micro-movements'. You're responding carefully to your own nipple and breast sensations and to the baby's communications. Her tiny hands are bare, and embracing either side of your breast or chest when she's relaxed and feeding.

Babies are sensitive little creatures, immensely vulnerable, and prone to fear and panic. It seems dramatic to say, but the newborn who can't find the breast is afraid of dying, since for him, milk is life. This is why getting in early with an offer of a feed if he seems at all hungry or upset is *so* important in the first days and weeks. You may even find your baby comes on best in a state of drowsiness or light sleep. Babies are smart, they want to co-operate. But when the sympathetic nervous system turns up high, the baby's reflexes become disorganised, and it is difficult for him to learn. Your soothing touch, your little songs, your reassuring words and murmurs over and over help calm him, so that his feeding reflexes switch on and do their job.

Gita: 'A midwife even tried holding him on.'

Gita and her husband are both engineers, and they tell me their story in a calm and matter-of-fact way, though they look exhausted. For the last 4 days they've been feeding their 6-week-old baby three bottles of formula daily, which has allowed them some desperately needed sleep. The baby's screaming has settled somewhat, too.

Because of a history of marathon feeds and extremely frequent night waking, I wonder even before watching a breastfeed if this baby is not transferring milk well and has been hungry, despite adequate weight gains.

Their baby was born by caesarean section, and received a flurry of attention from the neonatologist and other staff in the first hour after the birth. When a midwife finally put the baby between Gita's breasts a couple of hours later, he stirred a little then continued sleeping.

Midwives came by every now and then throughout the next 24 hours, giving Gita a hand to sit up, but the baby was very sleepy and didn't show much interest in the breast.

'A midwife even tried holding him on a few times,' Gita tells me. 'She was gentle, I liked her. She just kept up this steady firm push on the back of his head. He would suck desperately for a bit, then begin back-arching and squirming and screaming.'

By the end of the first 48 hours, Gita dreaded feed-times, which, needless to say, she put off as long as she could. The baby screamed for long periods, a terrible wavering baby-lamb cry. By the end of the third day, he'd screamed so much he was hoarse, his cry just an awful rasp. Now, the nurses and midwives were earnestly trying to help. They put pillows on her lap; they taught her a cross-cradle hold, with her hand and fingers around his neck and upper back and shoulder, lifting him to the breast on the opposite side the way they'd been trained. A lactation consultant suggested Gita recline back and use 'the baby-led approach', so that he ended up lying diagonally across her tummy. When the baby finally did take the breast, Gita's nipples began to hurt. She was discharged the next day, even though she felt panicked about feeds, the baby was still losing weight, her breasts were engorged, and her nipples stung badly in the bra.

She endured two heroic days at home, with excruciating nipple pain and a baby who fretted and back-arched and cried throughout every feed and who screamed whenever he wasn't sleeping. Gita's husband hovered, changing nappies, bringing her water and meals, doing the housework, walking with the baby crying in his arms, trying to project a cheerful calm though his gut churned at times, too.

By day six, things were obviously horribly wrong. They made an urgent appointment with the GP, who advised supplementing with formula and referred Gita to a private lactation consultant.

Things calmed down a little, thanks to expressed breast milk. The lactation consultant advised Gita to pump for a quick burst of no more than 10 minutes, eight times a day (or really just whatever she could do) with a hired, hospital-grade, double electric pump, combined with hand expressing, and she found this reasonably manageable. Once her nipples had healed, the baby learnt to come on to the breast with the help of nipple shields, and Gita changed to cradle hold during feeds, with the baby's head resting on her forearm on the same side from which she was feeding. Soon, she felt ready to stop seeing the lactation consultant, since the visits were expensive.

By week four, Gita had managed to wean herself and the baby off the nipple shields, and was no longer pumping. He was still unhappy most of the time. He'd stay on the breast for 60 minutes or more if she let him, and the nights were regularly broken every hour or so, but she was proud that she'd managed to continue breastfeeding.

Then last week, one of her health professionals advised her to use more formula in the evening, in the hope of improving the nights. This seemed to work. The health professional also advised her to space out the breastfeeds so that the baby's tummy would 'stretch up' to take bigger volumes, and not need filling as often. The baby began screaming even more, if that was possible, and Gita and her husband began to use more formula to keep the days manageable.

I ask if I can watch a feed, and Gita obliges. She has been in the habit of supporting the baby with a pillow in her lap, but I explain that this often interferes with good positional stability and I help her to find another way.

'Actually, that feels better already,' she says in a while, pleased. The baby is relaxed and swallowing, and she feels no pain.

'You've been doing a marvellous job, after such a rough start. We should be able to sort this out. But it would explain why he wants to breastfeed so much, you see. He's still not been transferring the milk efficiently, with lots of breast tissue drag.'

When I examine inside the baby's little mouth, I observe he has normal capacity to move his tongue and normal frenula under his tongue and upper lip. (The frenula can be very different from baby to baby but still normal.) His tongue is rather short, his chin is rather delicate, and his palate is on the high side, but these are normal anatomic variations.

Gita and her baby's difficulties are an example of what's known as the 'butterfly effect'. A small experience early on can completely change the trajectory of the mother and baby's feeding relationship, with a large and unpredictable effect down the track. This baby, who'd already had a slow start due to birth complications, developed a negative association with the breast once force was used. To make things worse, he couldn't relax at the breast once he was on due to breast tissue drag and positional instability, resulting in engorgement, nipple pain, and ongoing stressful feeding experiences.

'I feel so bad about using formula,' Gita says, her eyes brimming.

Her husband quickly intervenes. 'Gita has given it everything,' he tells me firmly. 'No-one could have done more.'

71

I nod my head. 'You've given it everything!'

It seems to me that formula in a situation like this is a rational and healthy response. I aim to help Gita accept her decision to supplement, so that she is not weighed down by the guilt and self-reproach that only makes everything worse. However, the well-intentioned advice to space out feeds and use formula fails to identify the underlying problem.

'You've been amazing in what you've done,' I tell Gita warmly. 'This sure is one lucky little boy!'

I continue to watch her feed, and offer strategies to improve fit and hold. We want the baby to relax deeply at the breast. And in the meantime, as I explain to her, with each passing week his jaw and oral structures will grow relative to the breast and become more efficient and practised, so there is every reason to think that it won't be this hard for much longer.

WHAT IF MY BABY PANICS AT THE BREAST?

If the baby's hunger is too ravaging and her need so desperate that her feeding reflexes can't organise properly, she becomes overwhelmed and slides into a crying loop. Avoiding this panic may mean you feed her first and delay nappy changes until after you're finished with the first breast, or you bring her to your chest when she is only just beginning to wake and still very drowsy.

Your job is to try to remain tender and calm, trusting that you and the baby will work it out eventually, but I know how hard this can be. When feeds aren't going well, the worry any mother feels about her baby's health and weight can be overwhelming. Your own sympathetic nervous system turns on high. The rising anxiety, the increased heart rate, the racing negative thoughts are all hardwired biological responses of a loving parent to signals of distress from the baby.

It's normal to feel anxious when you are trying something new or learning new skills, even more so when what you want to learn is deeply important to you. It may not be possible to get rid of these bad feelings and anxious thoughts with positive thinking. In fact, the evidence shows that trying to eliminate the unpleasant thoughts and feelings that accompany a new endeavour often makes them worse. What matters is our *relationship* with our thoughts and feelings, and what action we take. This is where some proven techniques from a modern form of cognitive behavioural therapy, known as ACT (Acceptance and Commitment Therapy) are helpful, and we'll discuss these in greater detail in Chapter 8.

If the baby panics and back-arches and flails at the breast, you can notice not only his communications of distress, but your own rising feelings of anxiety, and the thoughts that run through your head ('I knew I wouldn't be able to do this', or perhaps, 'I'm a failure as a mother'). The first step to managing your own distressed thoughts and feelings if the baby isn't coming on to the breast is to become aware of them – to *notice* what's happening inside your mind and body, and to normalise it. Your anxiety and despair are completely understandable.

Then move your attention into your body. Consciously relax your muscles and breathe deeply, and begin to pay attention to other aspects of the present moment, like the scent of the baby, how he screws up his eyes and flushes red and screams and seems to think the world is ending when you know very well it's not – how exquisitely tiny he is.

Anchor your attention in the present moment, and then *expand* your attention, allowing your own distressed thoughts and feelings to run through your head like a radio in the background – not fighting them, but not focussing on them or getting caught up in them, either. Notice the room you're in, the sounds you can hear in addition to the baby, the world outside the window.

If the baby is persistently too upset to feed, you might stop trying until he is calmer. Think how you might nourish his senses with a change of environment or by snuggling him in skin-to-skin, to help dial him down. If you have one, and the weather's manageable, you could try going out on to the verandah to lie in a hammock together, and let the gentle swaying, the sounds of the birds or the street-life and the breeze on your skin calm you both.

I don't mean to make this sound easy, because it's not, but it gets easier with practice. It might be helpful to know that you are practising skills proven to protect mental health and which will stand you in good stead throughout the rest of your life.

BABIES ARE NATURALLY SLEEPY AFTER FEEDS

Once your milk comes in around the third day, your baby's jaw begins to chug up and down with feeds, face and mouth buried in breast, eyes wide, and you hear the swallows, those miraculous bursts of suck-swallow-suck-swallow-suck-swallow-suck-swallow. She drinks you in. For her, breast is life. Breast is home.

Babies feed in an intent slow steady rhythm, like the slow beating wings of the currawong, like a mother's heartbeat. An efficient feed has bursts of regular audible swallowing, followed by a rest, followed by bursts of regular swallowing. It's worth watching what a normal newborn breastfeed looks like, so you know.

When your baby is plugged in, pressed up into you, her face buried in breast, those tiny nostrils might seem flattened against your flesh. If she really can't breathe, slide her bottom away from the breast, millimetre by millimetre towards her toes, so that her head tips further back, but her nostrils usually allow air in even when her face seems to disappear into the mound of your breast.

As the amount of milk flowing from breast to baby decreases, the concentration of cream increases. As we have seen, fat entering the small intestine switches on cholecystokinin, the hormone of satiety. The sensation of the tummy being stretched and full, whether from breast milk or formula, ramps up the rest-and-digest part of the baby's nervous system. Suckling satisfies the baby's hunger for sensory stimulation, too, as we will discuss in the next chapter.

The enveloping sensory bath of physical closeness and eye-contact releases oxytocin, triggering feelings of relaxation and safety. These powerful biological processes typically send the baby to sleep at the end of a feed, whether at the breast or bottle, particularly if the baby has already been awake for a while and his sleep pressure is rising. Even as adults, we might feel drowsy after a good meal: we call this 'postprandial somnolence'. In babies, sleepiness at the end of feeds is a prominent biological event, repeated frequently, day and night.

So at the end of a good satisfying breastfeed, after the suck-swallow-suck-swallow-suck-swallow, after a bellyful of milk subtly flavoured by the mother's recent meals, after the creamy suck-suck-suck-suck-suck-suck-swallow of dessert, the baby falls off the breast like a fat ripe fruit, little tummy swollen, and often sinks into sleep. Or he falls off the bottle asleep after a carefully paced bottle-feed, delivered in the same high-oxytocin package of physical contact, caresses and eye-contact. Then his little eyes dart sometimes under the half-closed lids, milk dribbles from his moist little mouth, a quirky half-smile flits across his dear elfin face in the first stage of sleep. This is a baby who is satiated, milk-drunk.

GETTING THE RIGHT FIT AND HOLD

In my work, I celebrate the kaleidoscopic diversity of body shapes found in mothers and their babies. Women's breasts may be delicately small, or large and pendulous, or any shape in between. Our areolas, which are more darkly pigmented than the surrounding skin, may be small and contained or a large generous spread. Nipples may be tiny and flat or large and long, even up to a couple of centimetres wide at the base. The shape of our upper arms, forearms and abdomens vary. Babies' mouths can be small or cavernous, palates high and bell-shaped or flat and broad. Most babies have receding chins, some more than others, and tongue length and the shape of its frenulum vary greatly.

With so much human variability, fit between mother and baby is a matter of experimentation – you just have to try out different ways of doing it. Babies adapt to their mother's anatomy and physiology and also learn, through experimenting, how to most efficiently extract milk from her particular breasts.

If you are tall and small-breasted, with a long willowy torso, the baby is likely to breastfeed best tucked horizontally across your body when you are semi-reclined, her belly against you when she is feeding. If you are short and large-bosomed and don't have much lap room, it may be necessary to recline back much further, still with the baby horizontal and flat against you above your belly, tucked right up under the other breast. Some women with long breasts and nipples that point downwards find that feeds go better at first lying down, and may need some skilled assistance to teach the baby how to fit on when they are sitting up. Mother–baby pairs are able to compensate at the beginning for the vagaries of fit and less efficient milk transfer with longer and more frequent feeds, until the baby's mouth grows a little, and fit becomes practised. This capacity to compensate is our in-built resilience and adaptability.

In the first few days of feeding, the baby's sucking often feels weird – a firm drawing pressure that is surprisingly strong. But if your nipples hurt, find help immediately, before damage is done. Painful nipples signal breast tissue drag and once damage sets in the pain can be excruciating. If there is discomfort, keep experimenting with the baby's position, her head on your forearm, tummy and pelvis in a tight rib-cage wrap, using micro-movements to eliminate any unpleasant nipple sensations.

Getting the fit and hold right for you and your baby takes experimentation, but in my work I use a new approach that we call the gestalt method. It is based on the latest ultrasound, vacuum and MRI studies. This simple stepped approach helps you prepare your body, turn on the baby's breastfeeding reflexes, and discover the power of micro-movements – that is, tiny one or two millimetre movements in various directions.

It's important not to put your hand or fingers on the back of your baby's neck or head, because this triggers a back-arching reflex. Once we are experienced, fit becomes dynamic and approximate. The bigger baby plays and wriggles happily at the breast and is endlessly distracted: the mother slips the baby on and off, casual and confident. Luxurious ease in breastfeeding arises out of neuronal circuitry consolidated by the careful early experiences of good fit.

Is my baby in the right position?

Sometimes the baby's head is positioned too far away from the breast's place of natural fall. The baby can't hold the breast in his mouth comfortably, or achieve pain free milk transfer because gravity is pulling the breast elsewhere: he is 'too far around the corner'. He has to tuck his little chin in to get to the breast. Sometimes this problem, so simply corrected, starts to emerge as the baby grows older (and longer), at 6, 8 or 10 weeks. I've seen mothers for whom breastfeeding starts to go downhill from 3 months or later, for this reason. For other women, the problem of fit and hold arises because the baby is being held up too high across their torsos, sometimes with pillows, when the breast and nipple naturally want to fall much lower.

Signs of poor fit include a nipple that:

- hurts
- is wedged after a feed
- swings down to point at the baby's chin when the baby comes off (or at some other place a long way from the mouth, depending on how the baby is held)
- has visibly broken skin.

Other signs of poor fit include:

- back-arching (because the baby can't find a stable position)
- breast refusal (because the baby can't find a stable position or is conditioned to feel distress at the breast)
- pulling off fretting
- crying and fussing at the breast (due to frustration and hunger from poor fit).

Samira: 'I've let her get into the bad habit of seeking comfort from the breast.'

Samira comes to see me with her second baby, who has a nappy rash. It's the first time I've met them. Samira tells me the baby is 12 weeks old.

'My 3-year-old has been sick and my husband is away, and now the baby has a nappy rash with these spots. Yesterday there were little white pustules,' she says.

The nappy rash is moderately red with spots around the edges, typical of a thrush infection. I recommend an appropriate cream. As Samira puts the nappy back on, she muses: 'I've let her get into the bad habit of seeking comfort from the breast.'

Samira's baby has always cried and fussed a lot. She feeds very often and for long periods, even for an hour, often wanting to return to the breast less than an hour later. I know, already, that this mother and baby have a problem of poor milk transfer.

The baby is gaining on average 100 grams a week, and Samira's previous doctor hadn't been worried. Babies often gain a lot in one week, very little in the next. Once the birth weight is regained and we are happy the baby is feeding well, it is the average over a period of a few weeks that is important. But when I weigh her today, the baby has dropped well over one percentile line since birth on the World Health Organization growth charts.

'I'm going to start spacing out feeds,' Samira adds. The baby gazes at me with her lovely black eyes, and begins a tentative smile.

'You're *very* beautiful, aren't you,' I say, smiling back.

'I get why you'd want to space out the feeds,' I say. 'She's feeding *so* much! But I think there's something going on to cause it, which we need to sort out so that she's back on track with her weight. Could I ask you to come in tomorrow and let me watch her breastfeed?'

I think to myself that this baby is already on the edge of unacceptably low weight gains, so spacing out the feeds will tip her over.

Sure enough, when she comes in the next day and I observe a breastfeed, Samira holds the baby diagonally across her torso, with the little hips and tummy tending to tip outwards. When her breast comes out of the baby's mouth, it drops low, so that the nipple points towards the baby's ear.

'Samira, if we could change your baby's positions through the feeds so that she is more stable, and so that the breast is falling into its natural position rather than being held up high in the baby's mouth, I think she would feed more efficiently.'

'Oh, really? Cool. What should I do?'

I encourage Samira to lean back a little, and to support the baby's head on her forearm, so that she can control just how the little face buries into her breast. I show her how to make the baby's position very stable, her chest and hips flat against Samira, supported by gravity, and to let the baby come to the breast, so that the breast is falling naturally.

'It feels weird,' she says, 'but I'll give it a go.'

I follow up a week later. The baby has gained 300 grams!

Samira tells me that her baby is much more settled. Feeds are still frequent, but much shorter. 'I hear her swallowing now, too!'

'Fantastic!' I say.

'It's funny, I thought I'd just got her into bad habits by feeding her all the time.'

'No, it wasn't bad habits! What you did was amazing! She wasn't transferring the milk efficiently but you responded to her and let her feed enough to compensate. That's why she had been getting by in her growth, at least until now,' I explain.

Samira listens quietly, nodding a little.

'So you can see why a lot of breastfed babies who are transferring milk inefficiently settle when they start to receive formula or solids, because they're suddenly more satiated!'

The baby coos and gurgles in Samira's lap, watching me with her alert black eyes. Then she reaches out with a wobbly little arm and grips Samira's long braid, hard, bringing it to her mouth.

'Ouch!' Samira cries, extricating her hair from her baby's determined grasp, and we all laugh.

HOW OFTEN SHOULD I BREASTFEED?

It's usual for babies to lose weight in the first days after birth, although if all goes well with breastfeeding, weight loss tends to be minimised. Very frequent feeding in that first week or two, maybe twelve times daily each breast (though I find it's best not to count), activates the prolactin receptors in your breasts, so that they produce milk efficiently in the months ahead. If we don't switch on an abundance of prolactin receptors at the very beginning, it becomes harder to build supply later on. Feeding frequently can make it difficult to get much else done in the days immediately after the birth, and ideally you will have support people on active duty, as you lay the foundations for easier days to come.

Frequent breastfeeding also prevents the horrible engorgement which characterised the post-birth period from the 1950s: breasts red and hot and rock-hard, two powder kegs about to explode into mastitis and fever and abscesses. When

I was a young doctor in the late 1980s, everyone favoured frozen cabbage leaves. Women sat forlornly in their hospital beds, weeping with pain, shivering from the thawing, wet vegetable leaves instead of having their baby skin-to-skin or at the breast. Like so many of the fashions that come and go in the care of mothers and babies, this one didn't help and possibly made things worse.

If a baby isn't able to take enough milk as that first week progresses, he either cries and fusses, or, paradoxically, becomes sleepy and uninterested in feeding, particularly if he is already a little jaundiced. (Jaundice is yellowing of the baby's skin and whites of the eyes caused by a build-up of a chemical called bilirubin which a newborn's liver can take a few days to process. About half of newborns have jaundice to varying degrees and it commonly resolves quickly if the baby breastfeeds frequently and milk passes regularly through the gut.) A baby with jaundice who is sleepy and not feeding well requires assessment by a health professional, because bilirubin can reach dangerous levels. Some reluctant little feeders are too sedated or too exhausted to cry, and again, health professional support is essential.

If all goes well, a baby settles down after the first couple of weeks into a rhythm of breastfeeds (even if sometimes clustered and very frequent), interspersed with periods of sleep and satiated contentment, in the context of good weight gain. He generally sleeps for blocks of two hours or so at night, sometimes more, sometimes less. He'll still cry and fuss on occasion, but on the whole, you feel in sync with your baby.

TWO TECHNIQUES WORTH KNOWING BEFORE THE BIRTH

Hand expressing

Knowing how to hand express puts you in control. You'll be able to avoid engorgement in the days after the birth if for some reason the baby can't take the breast.

The amount of milk you hand express or pump won't tell you anything about your supply, though, since the amount of milk women can express varies enormously, regardless of their actual milk production. Your supply is best protected by responding to your baby's cues with frequent breastfeeds, and seeking help for any underlying problems that emerge.

Softening tight areolae

If the areolae are tight and swollen due to intravenous fluids during labour or due to milk engorgement, and the baby can't latch on, it's helpful to know that you can soften them by applying fingertip pressure. Press the tips of your fingers together like a tulip into the areola and hold them there so that the gentle pressure disperses the swelling and softens the tissue, then bring the baby to the breast. This technique is called Reverse Pressure Softening.

Is my baby getting enough milk?

As the days pass, it can be difficult to know if your baby's frequent feeds are normal, or a sign of underlying problems. It's normal and healthy for newborns to feed twelve times each breast in a 24-hour period, and to sometimes want to feed again within an hour or less of the end of the previous feed. But a pattern of consistently returning to the breast within an hour or less with very little break for the mother day and night is referred to as 'marathon feeding', and is a reason for concern. A baby with poor milk transfer may have good urine and stool output, because she and her mother are compensating bravely, but she shows the following signs:

- consistently feeds for longer than 30–40 minutes (excluding nappy changes and other breaks)
- lacks the frequent bursts of audible swallows which demonstrate active milk transfer
- rarely falls off the breast satiated and drowsy
- is not gaining weight particularly well even though feeding often
- fusses and frets and cries when not feeding or sleeping
- sleeps for short periods at night (wakes frequently) due to hunger.

If you feel out of sync with your breastfeeding baby, and she is showing some or all of these signs, it is important to see your midwife, child health nurse, GP or lactation consultant for an assessment.

Megan: 'She's never been this settled during a feed before!'

Megan's 9-week-old baby has been diagnosed with reflux and is taking Losec. Feeds still last 45 minutes or longer, not including breaks, with the baby back-arching and fretting at the breast, and are distressing for both of them. Megan had early nipple pain but this resolved after a couple of visits to a lactation consultant. She believes the baby pulls off and back-arches because of pain in her oesophagus.

I watch a feed, and the problem is immediately apparent. There is a great deal of breast tissue drag when the baby feeds. The baby's mouth is too high and too far off to the side, relative to where Megan's nipple and breast want to fall.

'I'm afraid it's her position,' I say.

Megan looks up at me in surprise. 'So what should I do?'

While the baby feeds from her left breast, I help Megan slide the baby's bottom off to the right – so far right it feels weird to her, with the baby's long skinny 2-month-old legs kicking way out there by her side. But in that position, as Megan leans slightly back in the chair, the baby's head supported by her forearm, little legs flowing out to her right, the baby feeds peaceably for the first time ever. She no longer fights to try to keep the breast from falling out of her mouth, but feeds quietly, suck-swallow-suck-suck-suck-swallow-suck-suck-suck-suck-swallow. They sit like that for a few moments as I enter some notes on their medical records.

Finally Megan looks up at me in astonishment. 'I can't believe it!' she exclaims. 'She's never been this settled during a feed before!'

I see Megan a few weeks later, for the baby's vaccinations.

The baby cries a lot less and is much calmer with feeds. She only occasionally back-arches and pulls off now.

'It's strange that everyone tells you the back-arching is because of reflux, or gut pain' she muses, 'when it's to do with a feeding problem.'

'I know,' I reply with chagrin. 'Never mind that we've invented bionic limbs and artificial hearts. Understanding the way normal babies feed is a last frontier in the medical sciences!'

NEVER USE FORCE WHEN FEEDING

Women have often told me over the years in quiet despair that when the baby won't feed, they try pushing her on the breast, stuffing it in; or they push the teat into a resisting little mouth to finish off the bottle. They are so anxious for the baby to regain her birth weight, and feel pressured to keep the calories up and to keep those dots tracking along the percentile line. But any force at the breast or bottle, even a well-meaning hand gently pressuring the baby's head towards the nipple or the bottle into the mouth, risks creating negative associations. Sadly, the old-fashioned 'ram and jam' method of helping mothers to breastfeed caused countless cases of breast refusal.

Of course, poor fit can also condition the baby into associating the breast with distress, leading to breast refusal. Whatever the cause, parents then have to witness the heartbreaking sight of a baby ravenously hungry and desperate to feed wavering over the breast, pulling off, back-arching, fretting and crying. The collision of these two powerful drives, the longing for milk and the negative associations, is overwhelming. The baby quickly disorganises into a long bout of screaming. The mother, frightened, might be tempted to force the baby onto the breast, living her days as she does in the shadow of the growth charts. The problem of lasting feeding difficulties between mother and child often begin here, in a mutual spiral of frustration and distress.

In fact, any pressure over meals throughout childhood, whether negative (force or punishment) or positive (praise and rewards, aeroplane spoons zooming into the mouth) may have unfortunate long-term effects, resulting in poor weight gain, or excessive weight gain, or anxiety around food. After 60 years of anxious, expert-driven over-control of family meal-times, we've finally learnt that parents need to relax about food intake. The little saying, 'Parent provides, child decides' is especially helpful. Taken back to the first 16 weeks of a baby's life, it means we offer the breast (or the bottle) on any occasion when peace and calm are even mildly disrupted, to see if the baby wants to feed.

We *can* trust our baby's biology. We *can* trust him to competently signal the need for milk (except, as we have seen, for babies who are ill, or newborns who are very drowsy and struggling to regain their birth weight). Sometimes this is referred to as the infant's capacity to 'self-regulate' milk intake at the breast or bottle, but it is really another example of the elegance of cued care: the baby communicates; the parents observe and respond as best they can; the baby learns over time that the world is fundamentally safe and responsive. This lays down neuronal circuitries that help shape the child's personality and psychological disposition for the rest of his days.

Tracey: 'She's always like this, crying and grizzling after a feed.'

Tracey brings in her school-age child who has a cough and fevers. She's on maternity leave and has brought her 3-year-old son and her 6-week-old baby with her. Tracey had been breastfeeding relaxedly in the waiting room, and continues doing so as I check over the 7-year-old. When she changes sides, I happen to notice that the lower half of the second breast is slightly red.

By the time I put down my stethoscope and explain that the 7-year-old's chest is clear, the baby has fallen off the second breast in a doze. Tracey stands up to attend to the 3-year-old, who has slipped off the footstool by the side of the examination couch and landed on his bottom. Tracy slings the baby up over her shoulder with practised ease, cuddles the 3-year-old for a moment, and then moves back towards the chair. The baby begins grizzling and trying to bob down to the breast. She does that strange downward lunge, throwing her body off her mother's shoulder, wobbling there at right angles, hanging precariously over her arm.

'It's fine by me if you want to put the baby back on the breast – I have notes to make,' I say.

'Oh, it's okay. She fell asleep after the first side. When I offered her the other she fell back asleep. She's not hungry.'

I casually point out the baby's insistent bobbing cue, downwards, to the breast.

'It's amazing the way babies have that built-in reflex to get them to the breast,' I remark.

'She's full,' Tracey repeats confidently, sitting down. 'She's had enough. She doesn't need a top-up.'

I know that Tracey is afraid to put the baby back on the breast for many reasons: for fear of overfeeding her; for fear of teaching her to always look for the breast; for fear that this would make her life so much harder than it already is.

'She's always like this, crying and grizzling after a feed,' Tracey explains. Then she stands up again and rocks and pats. 'She might sleep for 5 minutes then she wakes and grizzles and cries. I have to walk and jog her, if I can, until she goes back to sleep. If the others need me I just put her down and let her cry. Sometimes she'll scream for a couple of hours.'

I listen supportively. This is a classic story of a baby who would be so much more settled if she was fed whenever she seemed to need it. Tracey, however, believes the 'colicky' behaviour is something normal she needs to tolerate until the baby grows out of it. I admire her resilience and stoicism.

'It was the same with the others – although the eldest had reflux, too,' she says with a grimace. 'Now *that's* hard work, I've got to tell you.'

I nod sympathetically. '*Very* hard work!'

'I've been told she definitely doesn't need more feeds. She's gaining about 160 grams a week.'

I don't try to talk her into feeding more frequently: she is obviously preoccupied by the needs of the other children, and anyway she hasn't asked for my advice. I can't help but think, though, how much easier another quick feed would be, compared to jogging and patting and managing a grizzly baby for an hour after a feed until the sleep pressure catches up.

Sure enough, Tracey was back within a few days with a nasty mastitis, shaking and sick with fevers. The lump was so hard and the symptoms so late by the time she came in, I wondered if there was an abscess. Fortunately, the ultrasound was clear. Her husband had to take a day off work to help out, and her sister flew up from interstate.

Tracey's experience shows how withholding the breast makes life harder, not easier. And for formula-fed babies, or those mixed feeding, the story is the same: responding to the baby's communications with a feed when the baby seems to want it makes life easier throughout the crying period, even though we've been told it will make life harder or harm the baby.

I see Tracey again to check that the mastitis is resolving, and during that consultation the baby again begins a funny little bob down her arm towards her breasts. This time, since she's sought my help, I am more proactive.

'It's a communication that the baby is ready to feed, you know,' I say.

'You're joking!' she says. 'She just fed!' We laugh at the funny behaviour.

'But we can never tell what the baby's little engine is needing on any particular day, so the best way to maintain the peace and keep the breasts well emptied is to feed whenever she seems to need it. You can just put her back on the same side if you think that's best. I know you've got a lot on your plate, but really, it's so much easier to have a contented baby! And it's one way to avoid getting mastitis again.'

Tracey regards me for a moment, and then shrugs. 'Well, I'll give it a go ... If you think it will be easier ...' She lifts up her blouse with practised ease and releases her nursing bra.

'But you don't have to take my word for it,' I say. 'Experiment over the next week or two and see what works best for you and your family.'

THERE'S NO SUCH THING AS A 'TOP-UP'

You might still hear talk about 'top-ups', but the breast is a dynamic, constantly active secretory gland. There's no such thing as a 'top-up', there's simply a feed. It may be very short, it may be long, depending on the baby's need and efficiency. Babies communicate their need to feed irregularly, whether they are breastfed or bottle-fed. Sometimes, like us, they want a little snack, sometimes a three-course meal. Sometimes they cluster feed, coming back again and again, especially in the late afternoons or evenings – which is often when babies cry and fuss more, and when caregivers find themselves running on empty, fatigued and desperate for a break, perhaps with the clamour of other children wanting food and attention.

Sadly, we have been taught that it is dangerous to be generous with the breast, that it will cause problems both short- and long-term, like reflux and obesity, that it will cause nipple problems and pain, that it will make the days even harder. When breastfeeding has already been hard – with a history of mastitis or cracked nipples or feeding refusal or infant crying – women often cannot bear the thought of breastfeeding more often. So we gamely jog around patting a grizzly baby, we work endlessly to distract him, we let him cry, managing our own stress as best we can. It's extremely hard work dealing with an unsettled baby. We develop mastitis because milk isn't being removed often enough. Our milk supply drops off, the baby's crying worsens, and breastfeeding seems even harder.

But in fact, once feeding problems such as poor fit,

poor milk transfer, or lactose overload have been sorted out, generous breastfeeding spares us most of this pain and anxiety; it also helps regulate the biology of the baby's sleep (which we'll discuss more in Chapter 7). In fact, generous breastfeeding makes life easier for everyone.

In the absence of other problems, babies become increasingly efficient sucklers, until they extract a surprisingly large amount of milk in increasingly short periods of time. They are also often distracted during feeds as they grow older – and that's no reason for concern, since they're not going to starve themselves, as long as the mother is happy to offer the breast flexibly. Usually women find that offering short, frequent, irregular feeds to keep the baby happy pays off, because the days are so much more relaxed and pleasant.

Jessie: 'She told me I was over-feeding my baby.'

'I went in to see a doctor and she told me I was over-feeding my baby,' Jessie says.

Her baby is 9 weeks old and had gained 750 grams in the fortnight preceding the check-up. Jessie had been breastfeeding whenever he signalled, which was perhaps every couple of hours, sometimes more, sometimes less (more often in the late afternoon and evening) to keep him settled. She'd let him take what he wanted from each side. He'd vomited quite a lot, slept for only half an hour or so at a time during the day, and always woke up wanting another feed.

'He's been pretty happy, though,' Jessie says, 'and the nights aren't bad. A few times he's even slept through.'

The biggest problem Jessie identified when she went in for that routine check recently was that his toddler sister kept distracting him during feeds.

The doctor told her to keep the baby on the breast for half an hour (15 minutes each side) in a room separate from the toddler if possible, then stretch out the feeds to every 3 hours. The doctor was insistent that this would make things easier in the long run. Jessie's new regime, however, had caused great disruption for the family.

'My nipples are hurting for the first time ever,' she says, 'because I'm trying to keep him on the breast longer, so that he'll fuel up and last better between feeds.' This is the reason she has come to see me.

'He's waking more often at night than he ever has, and he's crying a lot. Sometimes it goes on for 40 minutes nonstop. He's miserable much of the day! It was never like this before.' Her toddler plays inexpertly with a large colourful tin spinning top at our feet. The baby, propped up in Jessie's lap, gazes rapt at the toddler and the spinning top.

'I feel that life's unravelling,' Jessie says uncertainly.

'You can't over-feed a baby at the breast,' I reassure her after I've finished examining the baby, taken a quick peek at her nipples (which are very faintly inflamed), and we are all seated again. 'And possetting is a lovely little mechanism for self-regulation.'

'I suggest you simply go back to what you were doing before – it seemed to be working perfectly well,' I add.

Jessie looks at me with relief. When I see her a few weeks later (the toddler has a splinter in her foot), she mentions that everything is fine again now with the baby.

'I don't care what anybody else thinks,' she says. 'My friends are all putting their babies on routines but it didn't work for us. They say it's about feeling in control but I feel much more in control feeding whenever he wants. It's not that the days are always predictable, it's just that they're so much more enjoyable!'

TONGUE TROUBLES

A small number of babies can't extract milk from the breast efficiently due to a true or classic tongue-tie. This is a tight membrane which runs from the tip of the baby's tongue to the floor of his mouth or lower gum, seriously restricting tongue movement. It may result in feeding difficulty, nipple pain, and infant crying. Even bottle-feeding might be hard, with gulping, dribbling, gagging and fretting. True tongue-tie is easily fixed with a snip of surgical scissors. Why risk damaging an exquisitely sensitive part of a woman's body, when a controlled nick of a membrane under the baby's tongue, which has no blood vessels or nerves in it, spares the mother physical injury and spares the baby hunger and distress?

This situation has to be distinguished from breastfeeding troubles that aren't so simply fixed. New studies show that good milk transfer depends on the vacuum generated in the baby's mouth, not the mobility of the tongue. The baby needs to be positioned so that his face is deeply and symmetrically buried into the breast, so that you can't see his lips. As the jaw drops, a vacuum is created, which gradually draws more and more breast tissue in, filling up his mouth. It's important that the breast tissue isn't being dragged and pulled away in another direction at the same time, due to poor fit and hold. Once a true tongue-tie has been taken care of, the most common cause of milk transfer problems or nipple pain is not tightness of the oral connective tissues, but fit and hold problems, which create breast tissue drag and affect how much breast tissue can be drawn in. Unfortunately, there is a recent fashion to medicalise breastfeeding problems and blame oral connective tissue variations, just as we have medicalised feeding difficulties in crying babies and treated them as 'reflux' or allergy in the past. These days, unsettled babies with feeding problems are often sent off for deep scissor or laser cuts into the normal (if highly variable) connective tissue which anchors the tongue, despite no proven benefits, despite the likelihood of significant pain. As we have seen, quick fixes, whilst tempting, often have side-effects down the track which we could never have imagined.

Katja: 'The pain is unbelievable.'

Katja tells me that her nipples hurt. Her 8-day-old baby is either screaming or sleeping, in half-hour cycles. She has tried and tried to breastfeed him, but her nipples had hurt from the very beginning and over the last 48 hours even the nipple shields don't help. She's been pumping. Her partner, the baby's other mother, has been feeding the baby the expressed breast milk. Katja confides that her nipples are a little flat.

'Maybe that's it?' she asks.

However, flat nipples mostly aren't the problem because babies don't feed from the nipple, they feed from a mouthful of breast tissue. When I examine Katja and her baby, I find that her bleeding, cracked, scabbed nipples and her screaming baby may be caused at least in part by a minor congenital abnormality. The baby has a transparent membrane running from the tip of the tongue to just behind the crest of the lower gum. The tip of the baby's tongue is pulled into an inverted 'V'.

'The paediatrician did say that there was a tongue-tie,' her partner says. 'But he said not to let anyone go near it. He told us that everyone will want to cut it but that we should absolutely leave it alone.'

Katja looks pale. 'I've got to say that the pain is unbelievable.'

'Women often say nipple pain is worse than labour!' I reflect, and she nods vigorously. I recommend a frenotomy. I give them handouts to read.

'It's entirely your decision,' I say, 'but let me know if you want to have it snipped. It's a very simple, painless procedure.'

Katja and her partner decide to go ahead, and come back later in the day. The practice nurse holds the baby secure, and within seconds I have released the frenulum with a snip of a pair of sharp surgical scissors. I mop up a drop of blood from under the tongue with a piece of sterile gauze.

Soon the baby is back in Katja's arms, and feeding avidly from a bottle of expressed breast milk. Often a baby goes straight onto the breast after frenotomy, but Katja's nipples need longer to heal. Later in the week, we'll do some fit and hold work.

HEALTHY BOTTLE-FEEDING

Even if you are exclusively formula-feeding, you can bring your baby close to your bare breast, or allow her to suckle for the burst of oxytocin it brings you both. Sometimes, in a relaxed situation where the baby is not driven by powerful appetite and desperation and nobody is trying to make it work, a baby who has refused the breast may come on.

One of the problems with formula-feeding in the past, we think now, is that we tended to pour in the milk so quickly, with so little sucking effort on the babies' part, that they didn't have time to register satiety. Their tummies stretched to hold more milk than they needed, contributing to a greater risk of obesity in later childhood. We weren't paying attention to the babies' cues during feeds, and relied on the clock rather than the baby's communications to time the feeds.

A bottle-feeding baby is likely to be more settled if you offer cued care. If you are using formula, give him more or less the total volume recommended daily, offering smaller amounts more frequently, when he seems to want it. The key is to *pace* the feeds, following the baby's lead.

Here's what to do:

- use a standard, narrow-base, slow-flow teat
- lay the teat flat on the groove between the baby's upper lip and nose so that the base of the teat touches his lower lip
- wait for his gape reflex
- gently tilt the teat into his mouth when he opens it, so that it rests against his hard palate

- tuck him in close and almost upright, only slightly tilted back
- make sure his little head and neck are extended back into the drinking position
- hold the bottle more or less horizontally (only the tip of the teat should be filled with milk)
- offer lots of eye-contact, cuddles and communication
- watch for the baby to communicate that he's ready to take a break (perhaps fifteen or twenty swallows) then leave the teat in his mouth but tilt the bottle downwards
- lift the bottle back up to horizontal when he starts to suck again
- swap sides during the feed
- finish the feed when he no longer starts sucking again after taking a break.

THE BURPING MYTH

Maybe someone has told you that your baby has gas, which is causing the crying, and you need to burp her better. The idea is that you pat or stroke the baby's back, with the baby either sitting in your lap, lying on her tummy over your lap, or drooped up over your shoulder. The tummy pressure and patting are supposed to help release the air from the stomach.

Tummy pressure will often cause possetting, of course. But burping up wind after feeds (or during feeds) isn't necessary, and certainly doesn't help resolve cry-fuss problems. Burping is a ritual that spread around the world with the British Empire, and isn't practised in most other cultures. In fact, babies belch up air from the stomach naturally, like you or me, regardless of the position they are in. Those babies who cry from gas have fermentation of lactose in the large intestine (not swallowed air in the stomach), as we've discussed.

Unfortunately, burping is not entirely harmless. It interferes with the baby's sleepiness at the end of a feed, waking the baby up and overriding the combined effects of sleep pressure, the hormones of satiety, and the parasympathetic nervous system. For this reason, burping interferes with the biological drivers of infant sleep.

Deepa: 'What do I do with what's left in the bottle?'

Deepa comes in to see me 6 weeks after her first baby was born by planned caesarean section. Although she wanted to breastfeed, the baby has never accepted the breast. At first Deepa pumped her breasts, courageously. I am constantly in awe of women's resilience and determination to give their baby their breast milk, against the odds.

Deepa's younger sister recently had a mastectomy for an aggressive breast cancer, and has been hospitalised in the last 10 days with a rare life-threatening reaction to the chemotherapy. Deepa's husband works very long hours and can't offer a great deal of practical support. Deepa has secured a full-time place in child-care, and has to return to work in the next month, or risk losing her job. Despite everyone's best efforts, the baby screams for long periods most days.

'Actually I weaned him last week. He's only on formula now,' she tells me. 'He still cries a lot, though.'

'How are your breasts?'

'They're okay, I didn't have any problems.'

'He's been very lucky that you've managed to give him so much breast milk for so long,' I reply warmly.

But this lovely woman, black hair piled carelessly up on top of her head, cotton sweater falling off a shoulder, is a bundle of nerves and grief. As she tells me that she can't even visit her sister with the baby, due to the risk of infection, tears slide down her cheeks, and she shoves a bottle of milk with a wide-based teat into his mouth. I would have done this too, no doubt, if my baby began grizzling loudly for a feed just as I was telling the GP about how I'm not sure I can cope any more.

We talk.

I watch the baby back-arch in her arms, pulling away at the same time as he sucks hungrily, panting and frowning and holding himself rigid at times, fists clenched or fingers splayed out anxiously. He seems to fight the bottle. Even when he is more relaxed, his back arches a little, thin arms dangling. Sometimes, if he pulls off and begins grizzling, she taps his lips firmly with the teat, or tickles his cheek near his mouth, which causes him to purse his lips and back-arch and turn away, limbs scrambling. Other times, she pushes the teat into his mouth anyway, and he starts swallowing. He coughs and gags and possets once or twice.

Deepa holds the baby tentatively, even diffidently, at a slight distance from her body. This is understandable, given the baby's distress around feed times. Also, Deepa herself is deeply worried about her sister's illness and terrified about returning to work next week. On top of everything, her elder sister and brother-in-law are visiting from India, and staying with her. She had hoped they might help more with the baby, but they have not had children themselves and aren't keen. Apart from anything else, it is apparent to me that this mother and baby are at serious risk of long-term feeding difficulties.

I find a standard, narrow-base, slow-flow teat to show her.

'Can I suggest you buy one of these on the way home? The one you've got is too broad at the base. I know everyone says it better mimics the shape of the breast, but in fact the curve to the base is too steep. Babies do better with a standard base.'

Then I show her how to gently lay the teat against the baby's chin and lower lip so that the bottle is almost at right-angles to the baby's face and the upper part of the teat is touching his lower lip.

'We'll wait for him to open his mouth so he doesn't feel pressured,' I say softly. And then his moist little mouth gapes wide, a little animal-baby responding by instinct to the gentle pressure on both lips. 'Now slip the teat into his mouth tilting it upwards so it rests against his hard palate.'

'Great!' I say encouragingly when she does so.

I help her rearrange the way she holds the baby, too, so that he is seated on the same side of her lap as the arm she holds around him, tucking him in close and almost upright, just slightly tilted back. Deepa cradles him, snuggles him up firmly against her body. He gazes up into her eyes.

'See? He loves to feel cuddled in, all surrounded, when he feeds. His arms can't flail about; his spine is curved forward a little.' I smile. 'See how he's looking at you? You can talk with him now while he feeds and smile at him and play little games and he will feel very relaxed!'

I watch in silence for a while.

I tell her to notice when the baby is ready to take a break, after perhaps fifteen or twenty swallows.

'Hold the bottle almost horizontal. It's important that we never force him to take more than he wants. Let him suck for 20 or 30 seconds then tilt the bottle down a little, leaving the teat where it is in his mouth. Let him have a rest whenever he looks at all puffed. Watch, wait, talk to him. Once he's caught his breath – you'll know because he starts sucking again – lift the bottle back up to horizontal.'

'Make sure his little head and neck are tilted back, because no-one can swallow if their chins are buried down in their necks.' I tuck my chin under as I speak, showing her how hard it is to open my mouth or swallow or even speak like that.

'A feed like this might take between 15 and 40 minutes, perhaps including breaks. It's like a little dance,' I say. 'You watch him for those signs that he wants to take a break. Or just guess when it's time. Let the feed ebb and flow, that's the way they like it. They can drink comfortably if they have lots of pauses and interaction and cuddles. The idea is to make feeding as relaxed and pleasurable as possible, for him and for you, too. You'll know he has had enough when he doesn't start sucking again or when he drowses off to sleep. When you go back to work, feeding can be your special time together. And you'll have to show the staff at the child-care centre how to do it right.'

'What about him swallowing air?' she asks.

'Babies don't swallow much air,' I explain. 'But if you hear loud air-sucking sounds, tip the bottle up slightly, so that the milk fills up the end of the teat. That's where it matters. The idea is to have him sucking on the milk, rather than letting it pour in with gravity.'

I notice when Deepa reaches over to rummage amongst nappies and wipes in the bag she's put on the floor at her feet, finding a cloth for the baby's spill, she leaves the bottle dangling from the baby's mouth like an over-sized white cigar, his little gums clamped down hard on the teat. I reach over to help, mentioning that the bottle always needs to be supported.

'The thing is, if he clamps down a lot like that, it would set up patterns of muscular tension around his tongue and jaw and neck, which this little one definitely doesn't need!'

She nods and smiles wanly, placing the teat against his chin and lower lip again, waiting for him to open.

'Ah! See? He knows what to do!' I exclaim.

'So what do I do with what's left in the bottle?'

'Given that it's formula, throw it out. If it was breast milk, you'd be able to re-use it within a few hours, but discard it after that.

'And don't forget to swap sides during a feed, too, so that you can both stretch a little, and so that his brain learns to use both sides of his body.'

The baby's eyes are closing. He is nestled in, and deeply relaxed.

'You could review the volumes he's taking on a weekly basis. If you think that he's regularly taking significantly more than the recommended amount of formula, we have to be sensible. You might have to work harder at spacing out his feeds.' I pause for a moment. The baby dozes and she doesn't tip the bottle up again, letting her precious little boy sleep.

MAKING THE DECISION TO USE FORMULA

When breastfeeding isn't going well, women often find themselves wondering how long they can persevere. Only you can know what is right in your situation. The one thing worth remembering is that once breastfeeding becomes enjoyable and easy, and it often does as the baby matures, both the days and the nights are likely to be less exhausting if you are breastfeeding instead of formula-feeding. Looking back, many women are grateful that they were supported by those around them to hang in there through early breastfeeding problems.

If breastfeeding seems overwhelming and the difficulties never-ending, it helps to live one moment at a time, one feed at a time, one day at a time ('I can do this for one more day, and then I'll reconsider') or even one week at a time ('I can do this for one more week, and then I'll reconsider'), dropping back into the present moment and letting go of fears about the future. Also, it doesn't have to be all or nothing – you can use formula *and* have the baby at the breast whenever you and the baby feel like it, just for the pleasure of it, without any pressure to feed.

With any luck, it won't be long before you find yourself enjoying low-effort, casual breastfeeds. But this doesn't always happen. When it's too hard and you know something has to change, when you decide it's time to put the baby on formula (or if you made the choice to use formula from the start), you might find your decision judged by others. You may then feel guilty or even ashamed, as if you've somehow failed though you are doing your very best. This is not helped by the fact that many mothers' support groups remain defined by feeding method.

This experience of guilt about formula-feeding – or the pain of being judged – causes unwarranted psychological anguish to countless women who, like their breastfeeding counterparts, all want the absolute best for their baby. I consider making judgements about other parents because of their feeding method or infant-care style to be very damaging, yet it permeates our society. It also conveniently shifts the focus away from the worrying fact that most health professionals – even those who actively promote breastfeeding – lack the training to prevent, or identify and help with certain kinds of breastfeeding problems, due to the lack of research in this field.

Formula-fed babies do not cry more than breastfed babies – in fact, research suggests that breastfed babies are more likely to cry and fuss in the West, due, I would argue, to the problems that we have discussed in this chapter, which so often remain undetected. The most important thing you can do to support your baby's good health and development is to relax deeply into meal-times, interacting with him, cuddling and enjoying him, whatever you feed your baby.

6

NOURISHING THE SENSES

The brain is a sensory organ, integrating the sensations that pour into the body through the skin, the eyes, the nose, the ear, the tongue and the joints so that our bodies can interact effectively with the environment. As we saw in Chapter 2, the baby's capacity for sensory processing develops exponentially during the crying period. Rich and healthy sensory nourishment from birth is vitally important for the best possible development of your baby's learning, memory, and motor skills. However, for historical reasons, some of the baby-care advice that is popular today unintentionally works against this early neuronal flourishing.

Back in the early 1900s, as the effects of the scientific revolution began to impact on everyday life in the West, doctors warned that the novelties of modernity (such as electric lighting, radio and telephone, trains and motor cars) impacted dangerously on children's nervous systems, causing increased brain activity and decreased sleep. The quickened pace of life and resultant overstimulation in childhood was, the experts of the time argued, a public health issue. To avoid this overstimulation of babies and children, doctors advocated strict schedules and rules for families and institutions, particularly concerning sleep.

As the 20th century progressed, experts maintained their anxiety about the effects of modernism and its overstimulation of developing brains. In the 1970s, for example, in Queensland, where I grew up, 'Mothercraft' was a compulsory subject for all adolescent schoolgirls. I still have my Mothercraft Project Book, though it's yellowing now, and its hand-outs explain that the baby's nervous system develops best in calm, unchanging surroundings, that we shouldn't rock or jig a baby up and down, and that we should never talk to the baby during feeds or at sleep time.

Today, as a direct continuation of these old 20th-century beliefs, babies in the English-speaking world may have physical contact with the caregiver for only a quarter of the day, much of that within the unchanging and boring four walls of the house, and receive very little vestibular stimulation (that is, stimulation to the sense of balance, which occurs during movements through space). Babies are put down to sleep in a cot up to four times during daylight hours in quiet, dimmed rooms. Each time, they might be expected to nap for up to 90 minutes. In further efforts to avoid overstimulation, the cot area may be stripped of toys, mobiles and wall hangings. Modesty capes are placed over the mother's breast and baby's head during breastfeeding, so that the baby isn't distracted by other sensory events. Cloths are placed over prams in the belief that this will keep babies calm. These days, even carriers have detachable fabric that can be fastened like a little awning to cover babies' heads and faces. Parents are warned ominously that overstimulation results in an overtired, fretful baby, who won't fall asleep. They are also warned that the overstimulated, overtired baby is learning bad habits which will affect behaviour and development in later childhood. The research, however, shows that none of this is true.

BABIES CRY FROM SENSORY BOREDOM

The fact is, *under*-stimulation poses a far greater risk to our babies' development than overstimulation, and many of our babies cry from sensory hunger. Babies crave the normal ebb and flow of human sounds and love environments awash with diverse sensory experiences. In particular, they crave the rich bath of diverse sensory stimulation that comes from the pleasure of interaction with a loving parent.

The safest place for a baby to sleep is in the same room as a caregiver, because the exchange of sensory data that occurs between caregiver and baby – even when we are not aware of it and the baby is sound asleep – wraps him in subliminal biological protection. The baby hears you, you hear the baby – even if it's just each other's breathing and other small sounds of physical presence. The safest place for your baby to sleep during the day is in the same part of the house you are in, near to you, surrounded by daylight and the healthy sounds of family life.

Because of the persistent belief that babies become

overstimulated and overtired with too much activity and social contact, parents are often told to stay at home and to get into a better routine if their baby is unsettled. When the baby signals with frets and grizzles and cries that he needs a change in sensory environment, parents are often taught to interpret these signals as 'tired cues', and to deprive the baby of stimulation. The baby cries even more, and parents are taught to read this as 'resisting sleep'. (That's not to say that some babies won't eventually fall asleep in these circumstances: it's just that there are usually much easier ways!)

The parent's body is the baby's primary source of sensory nourishment, especially for newborns, available to the baby wherever they are, inside or outside the house. If you keep an eye on the baby for cues, if the baby starts to look upset, if the baby begins to fret and grizzle and cry – back-arches, pulls away from yet another relative's or friend's doting attentions – then that's the time to simply respond to these communications and bring the baby back to your arms. In this way, as the weeks pass, a baby can explore the world, be richly exposed to the diverse sensory nourishment she craves, and yet return to the familiar calming, enclosing sensations of your body and the accompanying soothing communications, whenever she needs. Decreasing sensory nourishment by spending more time in the home makes many babies *more* unsettled, not less.

Sally: 'She gets overstimulated, which makes her overtired, so she won't sleep.'

In the waiting room, Sally pushes a pram draped with a heavy black cloth back and forth, back and forth. I hear a baby grizzling inside, on and on.

She wheels the pram into the consulting room and before long I learn that trying to get her 14-week-old firstborn back to sleep means rocking the pram with the cover down for up to 45 minutes, four times a day.

'She won't sleep any other way,' Sally explains despairingly, still rocking the pram in the confined space of the consulting room as the grizzling continues. My heart goes out to her, and I feel sad that she has been given advice that makes her days so miserable.

'She gets overstimulated, which makes her overtired, so she won't sleep,' Sally explains. 'When I was breastfeeding, she used to feed and feed,' she says. 'I nearly went mad. I was waiting for her to go to sleep, and all she'd do was feed.'

She tells me she has weaned the baby now, and has used the pram-rocking strategy over the past month to stop the baby getting into the habit of going to sleep in her arms.

We talk for a bit longer and when I judge the moment is right, I dive in. 'I know this sounds unbelievable, given all that you've heard, but babies are actually more settled if they receive richly varied sensory stimulation.'

She looks at me in disbelief. 'What do you mean?' she says. (I suspect the only reason she doesn't walk out is that she's heard I get good results.)

'There's a certain kind of stimulation that's not good for anyone,' I explain. 'We know from research with premmies, for instance, that radios blaring and fluorescent lights 24 hours a day are not good for them. The same might be true of TVs left on near the baby all day, for example, and those sleep machines that make 'white noise' worry me, too. But the ordinary sounds and sensations of family life are extremely nourishing for a baby's developing brain, even when they are sleeping.'

I explain to her that even if there isn't an underlying feeding problem, a baby who is hungry for rich environmental stimulation might feed a great deal if there's nothing more interesting going on, because it does give her a great big dose of delightful sensation.

Sally is listening intently, and her expression is softening.

'Feeds profoundly nourish the baby's nervous system, as well as provide life-giving nutrients, and will be the easiest and most satisfying way to calm most babies once any underlying feeding problems have been sorted out. But if you get out of the house and fill your baby's days with all sorts of other activities, things to see, feel, hear, smell, lots of vigorous movement, lots of social interaction, then the dependence on feeds and physical contact as the only sources of rich sensation diminishes.'

'It makes sense ...' Sally says, hesitating.

We talk a bit more and, in the end, Sally agrees to try an experiment – just for a week. If the baby doesn't drop off to sleep after a short time, she agrees to act as if her baby doesn't need to sleep right then and to get on with her day, trying to do all the errands and social things she wants to do for herself with the baby accompanying her. We also talk about paced bottle-feeding, so that she can use feeds more often to satisfy the baby's hunger for sensation, within the approximate bounds of the recommended volumes.

When we meet the following week, Sally is buoyant. 'It's been the best week I've had since she was born!'

'Oh, I'm so pleased!'

'It's been so much easier just taking her with me,' she says, 'but I'm still worried that I'll pay a price down the track.'

'Yes, people often worry about that,' I say. 'But if we look at the evidence, efforts to *make* the baby self-settle in the first 6 months of life have no effect at all on the baby's sleep and behaviour later in childhood.'

'I was also a bit worried because she was 50 ml over what's she supposed to have three days in a row.'

'To tell you the truth,' I say, 'I'm not worried about that at the moment. We'll keep an eye on her daily volumes over time.'

FEEDING SATISFIES TWO HUNGERS

You can see, then, that babies cry from two kinds of hunger: the hunger for milk and the hunger for sensation. The hunger for sensation is not as life-threatening as the hunger for milk, but is nevertheless a powerful biological drive, still radically misunderstood in our society for the historical reasons I've discussed.

In the crying period, on the whole, it is difficult to separate the hunger for milk from the hunger for sensory nourishment. If we look at maps of the newborn's sensory and motor cortex, a large proportion relates directly to the mouth and tongue. The primordial drive to suck satisfies the baby's hardwired cravings for both milk and sensation.

Breastfeeding is often said to be a kind of analgesic, but the calming effect of breastfeeding during vaccination, for example, can't be explained by what's in the milk, since digestion doesn't happen instantly. It's the flood of sensations that accompany breastfeeding: the rippling suck-suck-sucking, the warmth, the firm pressure on the joints, the satisfaction of milk filling the tummy. For all of us, physical discomfort is less noticeable when the body is drenched in pleasurable sensation – a warm bath, for example, or a massage. Bottle-feeding, too, has the potential to offer your baby the same calming and analgesic effects of cuddles, eye-contact, little soothing words and caresses.

In the early months when the baby fusses, we don't want to spend too long finding out if cuddling and rocking will do, because once the baby moves into a full-blown cry she will find it very difficult to feed, even if that is what she wanted. If parents trust the competence of the baby's cues, and offer milk early and often, both sensory and nutritional needs are attended to.

A HEALTHY SENSORY DIET

From around 6 months, you'll be thinking more and more about how to balance your child's nutrient intake with a healthy intake of solids. But it's particularly important to make sure that your baby's *sensory* diet is balanced and healthy from birth onwards, in order to nourish your baby's neuronal flourishing. A healthy sensory diet is achieved by:

- responding to your baby's communications, as best you can given your own particular circumstances
- sorting out any underlying feeding problems (whether

with breast milk or formula) so that feeds efficiently satisfy the two hungers

- interacting with your baby regularly throughout the day, experimenting with your touch, voice, and facial expressions to find what style of communication your baby enjoys
- offering a sensible, middle-of-the-road amount of physical contact each day, with the help of those around you, including older siblings
- focussing on enjoying your own days outside the house (or bringing social activity into the house) with the baby accompanying you
- offering the baby opportunity for diverse positions in relation to gravity, including tummy time.

We've already dealt with the first two of these in the previous chapters. Let's look at the others now.

Physical contact

Holding and carrying your baby is a powerful bolus of rich sensory input – touch, pressure, movement, scents, sounds, the warmth of skin – all of which help lay the foundation for healthy neuronal development. There's no other kind of input that stimulates so many senses all at once in such a healthy way, other than feeding, which combines the benefits of physical contact with the deeply satisfying sensations of sucking and of milk in the tummy. And of course, if your baby is in close proximity, it becomes easier to interact with her in countless subtle ways – a moment's eye-contact here and there, a little smile, a funny face, a brief caress, warm words as the baby coos back – all of which ramp up the sensory (and therefore emotional) exchanges which nourish the development of the baby's brain.

Baby-carrying devices, to tie offspring to the hairless, pouchless adult, are among the earliest documented tools used by humans. In addition to the sensory nourishment of physical contact, tying the baby on so that you can move about comfortably and continue with your daily tasks is a wonderful way to expose the baby to a kaleidoscope of changing visual micro-environments. A good carrier supports the baby's head, neck and spine safely, while leaving the adult's hands free.

If you start using a baby-carrier down the track, it might take your baby time to adjust, so it's best to use it for at least short periods every day right from the beginning. Used preventatively, slings and carriers (or baby-carrying devices) reduce unsettled behaviour. I recommend only wearing a sling or carrier that supports the baby in a vertical position against your chest or back, because a baby curled up in a sling worn diagonally across your body with her chin tucked in towards her chest is at risk of airway obstruction. Babies need a carrier that supports their bottoms and thighs in the 'frog' position, hips flexed and spread apart, to protect hip health, and you need a carrier with good waistband support, so that your hips take the baby's weight and your back and shoulders are protected from drag.

A baby who is more easily frustrated due to personality or because her stress response is set on high or both, needs to be drenched in as much multi-dimensional sensory experience as possible. The quickest and most effective way of achieving this is against the caregiver's body. Some people warn that the use of carriers sets up bad habits, teaching the baby to expect constant physical contact. Their advice is well-meaning – they, too, want to protect mothers in particular from unnecessary exhaustion and unreasonable expectations. But managing a restless, dissatisfied or crying baby is extremely hard work – much harder than carrying a reasonably content baby in a carrier on your chest or back for some of the day.

I like to imagine there is a little tank inside the baby which stores up sensory experiences. We can fill up the baby's sensory cup to overflowing through physical contact whenever we've got the strength for it, or when others are around to help. Older siblings, too, can be a rich source of physical contact. The baby who is preventatively fuelled up with generous doses of sensory nourishment will be better able to tolerate periods of minimal stimulation when no-one else is around to help, when our energy is low, when we need the baby to tolerate the car capsule or lie happily on the floor in the lounge room under a mobile without our attention for a time.

Sometimes parents are reluctant to carry the baby in their arms while they do other tasks due to concerns about lack of neck support. Obviously little brains and spinal cords can be terribly and permanently damaged by violent handling or shaking, but the ordinary, sensible movements of a loving parent carrying a baby, even though the baby's little head and neck are somewhat floppy at times, will only help to strengthen the baby's muscles and coordination, not do harm, and we don't need to be frightened of it.

A middle-of-the-road approach is as effective as attachment parenting

I don't necessarily promote what's popularly thought of as 'attachment parenting', where you might sleep with your baby and carry or hold her most of the day. But I am certainly an advocate of generous and ample breastfeeds or, in the crying period, of frequent, carefully paced bottle-feeds, whenever the baby seems to want them because this makes life easier for families overall. I'm also an advocate of abundant interaction with your baby, just for the pleasure of it.

I'm not against attachment parenting either; it's just that I find most families do best if they aim for balanced, middle-of-the-road amounts of physical contact with their baby, in a way that is workable for them, at the same time as they focus on creating a rich and satisfying social life that includes the baby. And there is evidence to support a moderate approach.

For example, a 2006 study compared three groups of new families: 113 in London, 74 in Copenhagen, and 57 who practised 'proximal care' (attachment parenting). The study defined 'proximal care' as holding the baby more than 80 per cent of the time between 8 a.m. and 8 p.m., frequent breastfeeding, sleeping in the same bed, and rapid responses to infant cries.

Proximal care parents had physical contact with their babies (whether they were waking or sleeping) on average 15½ hours in a 24-hour period. London parents had physical contact with their babies (awake and sleeping) on average 7 hours in a 24-hour period. The Copenhagen group were in the middle, with just under 10 hours of physical contact with their babies in a 24-hour period.

London parents were more likely to use routines and feed spacing; Copenhagen and proximal care parents were more likely to offer cued care. At 12 weeks, both proximal care and Copenhagen parents slept in the same bed at least part of the night on five nights a week, compared to one night a week for the London parents. Eighty-five per cent of the proximal care and 70 per cent of the Copenhagen babies still exclusively breastfed at 12 weeks, compared to only 37 per cent of London babies.

This study found that the proximal care and Copenhagen babies fussed and cried for about the same amount of time over a 24-hour period at 10 days and 5 weeks of age, but the London babies fussed and cried *twice as much*. Other studies support the finding that Danish babies cry less. It's very helpful to know that a sensible, middle-of-the-road approach is likely to have the same effect on crying and fussing as a more classic attachment parenting style, and I believe it's important that you decide what works best for you, experimenting and responding flexibly to your own unique situation and child.

Getting out of the house

It is important to plan days outside the home that are satisfying for yourself, as this provides other opportunities for your baby to have lots of sensory stimulation. This might seem confronting if you have received advice to stay quietly in the home and get the baby into good sleep routines because he is unsettled. But remember that even in societies that practise lying-in periods after birth, new mothers and their babies live intimately with others, in the midst of comings and goings and a busy communal life, quite different to the sensory and social isolation of our big homes in the West, where even windows, which once brought the outside world in close, now tend to be a long way across the room and closed for temperature control. We need to adapt and go out into the world to create the rich sensory and social engagement that our baby's brain and our own spirit needs.

As we have seen, one of the best ways to make life easy in the crying period is to use the breast or carefully paced bottle-feeds generously, whenever your baby seems to be signalling hunger or unhappiness. However, if you are too house-bound, you may find that the baby relies on feeds as the only source of sensory nourishment in an otherwise unmoving, unchanging, quickly boring environment, and this may create a downward cycle of frustration and distress for both of you.

If you are out and about with the baby, enjoying morning tea with friends, walks in the park, a visit to a family member, yoga for mothers and babies, or playgroup, he will revel in the rich sensory bath. 'But what about his sleep?' I hear you ask. In the next chapter, we will see that in the context of satiety of both milk and sensation, we can trust babies to take whatever sleep they need during the day without us having to try terribly hard. This is one of the reasons why second and third babies are often so much more settled: they simply have to fit in around school and kindy drop-offs and pick-ups and the activities of busy family life, and parents find themselves less worried about their newest addition's daytime sleep.

Time on the tummy, time on the back

Providing generous opportunities for motor development is an important part of a balanced sensory diet. Since the early 1990s, we've been sleeping babies on their backs because this offers vital protection against sudden infant death syndrome (SIDS). Physiotherapists have become concerned, however, that babies are receiving less opportunity to develop core strength and musculoskeletal coordination in response to the pull of gravity. The experience of diverse positions in relation to gravity nourishes the baby's nervous system.

For example, a baby needs plenty of opportunities to lie on her tummy from birth, to develop core stability and integrate muscle movement and strength in the upper back, shoulders and neck. It might only be for a minute or two at first. We don't want to condition her into disliking this position, so if she's signalling she's had enough don't persist. It's important to keep offering it a number of times a day, though, perhaps at nappy changes, until the time comes when she is regularly rolling herself over (from around 6 months of age). You could give her tummy time lying on your chest or belly, too, so that you can talk with her and make the moment enjoyable. You could get down on the floor in front of her and play with her. There's no need to pull a newborn's arms forward when you put her down on her tummy: she'll want to be curled up with her legs and arms tucked under her in the foetal position at first. In time she'll find a way to bring her little arms forward by herself and by 3 months she'll lift herself up on her elbows and forearms, doing what look like little baby push-ups as she gazes at the world.

Babies can also be carried on their tummy over your arm. My own babies loved this position, I think because it's such a sensory workout. They enjoyed being moved around through space (vestibular stimulation), close to my body (warmth, touch, deep pressure, aural and olfactory stimulation), being able to see what was going on in the world (visual stimulation) – at the same time as they developed core stability in response to gravity (sensorimotor stimulation).

Particularly after the first few weeks, your baby is more likely to enjoy time alone on the floor without your attention if you put her down on her back without the nappy, to kick or (before you know it) to explore her hands – the lovely feeling of the air on her little bare bottom and the pleasure of nappy-free movement is likely to keep her entertained for a while. If you don't want to take the nappy off, leave it loose around her waist, because moving freely on her back during floor-time allows her opportunity to develop core stability. Babies never need pillows, just a mat on the floor.

The incidence of plagiocephaly (flattening of the skull) has dramatically increased since we began sleeping babies on their backs. If we change the position of the cot or bassinet or mat regularly from birth so that the baby doesn't always lie with her head on the same side looking towards the door, we may be able to prevent the mouldable little skull flattening on one side. If the baby does develop a plagiocephaly, it's important to talk it over with a paediatric physiotherapist or osteopath, and your doctor. Flattening of the skull doesn't cause harm and the baby generally grows out of the worst of it, but the best strategy is prevention, using different locations when you place your baby on her back during the day for any length of time.

Kris: 'The paediatrician thinks the squirming is due to pain from reflux.'

Kris, the mother of an unsettled baby who is nearly 4 months old, has been feeling lonely and isolated. She has no family locally, and all her friends are at work during the day. She is a single mother. The baby's father takes the baby for 48 hours every other weekend. The paediatrician, who'd diagnosed gastro-oesophageal reflux disease when the baby was 6 weeks old and commenced him on a proton pump inhibitor, has recently recommended that Kris give him paracetamol when he seems especially wriggly. Kris has come in for a second opinion.

'The paediatrician thinks the squirming is due to pain from the reflux,' she reports.

I look over at the baby in his stroller. It's true that he is squirming a lot. He's also grimacing, flailing around restlessly and sometimes back-arching. It seems to me he could be hungry for milk, or he could be hungry for more sensory stimulation. Kris isn't picking him up, because she thinks it's just the reflux that's bothering him.

'And anyway, he's not hungry, he only fed an hour ago,' she observes.

I inquire carefully into her relationship with the baby's father, wondering if he can be further involved, but the situation is painful, involving legal action, and I see that my role is to focus on Kris's immediate needs and those of her baby.

After our discussions, she sets up a plan which includes making a point of holding the baby against her with firm physical contact at times throughout the day, even squeezing his limbs firmly as she feeds and plays and has fun interacting with him, and particularly when she notices he's restless; feeding him more or less whenever he cues for it; introducing the use of a back-carrier (which she could suggest that his father uses, too) for more vestibular activation at the same time as he receives visual stimulation; joining a yoga group for mothers and babies;

and taking various other little steps to get out of the house more often.

I see Kris 2 weeks later, and she has a lovely story to tell me. She made a trip into town and met two old ladies who were floored by the sight of her child in the pram.

'They were *really* old,' Kris says, 'maybe in their eighties. And they just couldn't get over my baby.'

She explains how they stood there for ages, clucking and smiling and telling her how beautiful he was. He responded by putting on a delightful performance, coos and gurgles. 'You should have seen him!' The young woman's eyes fill with tears. 'I think it really made their day. I'm not just saying that.'

'I'm certain it did,' I reply.

'They said I was obviously doing a fantastic job.'

'That's obvious to me, too,' I say.

I can imagine it. Two very old women walk with death perched on their shoulders like a wise old bird – death their friend, death their companion – and they know with stunning clarity the miracle of new life, the baby. They know how the new mother needs to be seen. So they step out of the shadows, they dispense admiration, they croon like old divinities bestowing blessings.

I remember how the warm smiles and encouraging words of other women, those benevolent strangers – not just the very old, but any woman who *knew* – succoured my days with small babies. But we can't receive this gift if we are locked inside the house.

I smile at Kris. 'It's great that you're getting out,' I say.

'And he hasn't been as restless and fidgety. He loves it when I hold him tight and stroke him. I'm thinking I'd like to stop the Losec.'

I hesitate. Certainly there is no reason to give her little boy paracetamol. But sudden withdrawal of proton pump inhibitors causes rebound acid secretion, even if they've been prescribed unnecessarily, so we need to wean him off slowly. I also think it might be wise for Kris to consolidate her new strategies for another couple of weeks before she takes this psychological leap. We are all of us, doctor and patient alike, affected by the power of the placebo, so taking a child off a medication that he doesn't need, but which everyone around him believes works, requires great sensitivity.

She agrees to talk this over with her paediatrician after I offer to give him a call and explain what we've discussed.

AN UNBALANCED SENSORY DIET

Certain kinds of sensory stimulation are unhealthy for the developing human nervous system. An unbalanced sensory diet contains disproportionately low levels of physical contact (e.g. long periods lying on the floor or in the cot, resulting in relatively few experiences of touch, movement through space, joint pressure, and visual diversity), or high levels of harsh, repetitive, enduring background noises, such as loud and heavy traffic day and night, or blaring TVs and radios left on around the clock, or flickering screens with constant rapid motion, or perhaps even large doses of 'white noise' (which people often use despite the lack of evidence that it helps settle babies).

In recent years, we have come to understand the importance of regulating levels of sensory stimulation in educational settings so that young children remain calm and alert and able to learn. Children who have learnt to shut down and become hypo-aroused ('zoned-out') in the face of stress may need more stimulation through physical activity if they are to become alert enough to learn well. Children who are hyper-aroused (impulsive and unable to focus) in the face of stress may benefit from less stimulation – that is, uncluttered environments and quiet work places so they become calm enough to pay attention and learn.

Unfortunately, I notice this important new work with older children in the classroom is sometimes misinterpreted to support the old idea that the 'overstimulated' ('overtired') baby needs to be taught 'self-regulation' through self-settling into sleep. But this new work is based on the premise that kindergarten or schoolchildren *learn to self-regulate through being emotionally regulated* by caring adults. The teachers read the individual child's physical and other communications, and act to decrease the stress levels experienced by that individual child, so that he is helped into a calm, alert state. How much more important is it, then, that we give advice that helps parents turn down a baby's sympathetic nervous system as far as possible, so that their baby is content, alert and able to learn to feed and process sensory input, so that he can lay down the best possible neuronal templates as a foundation for the rest of his life?

We may not be able to help our baby cry and fuss less, but we can take heart from the knowledge that the crying is unlikely to have any long-term effects. In the complex and dynamic system of the family, hundreds of factors bolster a child's resilience as the parent and child go through life together, day after day, year after year. Regardless of how unsettled the baby is and regardless of the strategies we choose to use in the crying period, children generally turn out just fine! Most babies and their families are remarkably resilient, and we can rely on this. What matters, from my point of view, is that we don't give advice, as health professionals, which inadvertently makes life harder for families! And advising families to *decrease* their baby's sensory nourishment does just that.

OTHER SENSORY STRATEGIES FOR UNSETTLED BABIES

Apart from the most important step of planning ahead to make every single day as satisfying for yourself as it can possibly be outside the home, it's useful to have other sensory strategies up your sleeve for a baby who is fussing. Often the aim is simply to calm the baby enough to feed or to drop off to sleep or both. Again, I'll offer some ideas, but it's important that you experiment and decide what's workable in your own unique situation.

Rocking

Vestibular stimulation (stimulation to the sense of balance by irregular movements through space) tends to result in a calm alert state, often observed when the baby is held in your arms or in a baby-carrier as you get on with the day. Slow, rhythmical vestibular stimulation fires neurones in the brain stem to turn down the sympathetic nervous system and calm the baby. This is why steady walking with your little one in your arms may be the most effective way to calm a baby who is too distressed and disorganised to feed. Even once a baby is overwhelmed by a crying loop, the nervous system can sometimes be calmed by strong repetitive vestibular stimulation in the one plane like this (i.e. by rocking). Many families use the time-honoured strategies of rocking chairs and hammocks to activate the baby's vestibular system.

Baths

Babies often love to feel immersed in the warm and soothing sensation of water, with the tactile and sensorimotor pleasure of kicking and splashing. Since I was committed to making life as easy as possible for myself, my own babies were still very young when I simply brought them into the bath with me. We enjoyed the luxuriant burst of tactile, vestibular, auditory and proprioceptive stimulation and all the delightful interactions that a bath or, as they grew a little older, a gently running shower offers. (I rarely bothered with slippery soap or cleansers of any kind on sensitive baby-skin – unless we were dealing with the effects of little accidents.)

Music

Playing music and dancing around with the baby gives him a quick shot of vestibular stimulation if he is fretting or crying, and gives you the pleasure of some physical activity, too. You may be surprised at how vigorous you can be (within sensible constraints!), and how much the baby likes it. Again, the time-honoured practice of singing lullabies soothes babies, and some mothers start singing when the baby is in the womb, so that the baby recognises and responds with calm to her songs after the birth.

Massage

In some Eastern cultures, baby massage has been a traditional infant-care strategy. The research shows that massage doesn't necessarily make babies more settled, but it might be something you want to try. Many babies prefer deep gentle squeezing of the arms and legs to whole-body stroking, which can be intrusive for some. (I've also seen many fine spotty rashes over the years caused by oils blocking up the baby's pores – sorbolene with 10 per cent glycerine avoids this.)

To my mind, a baby who is squeezed and gently bumped around close to a caregiver's body is already having a massage, and once you and the baby have the hang of it, putting the baby in a carrier is so much easier than planning a special massage experience. Not only is the baby automatically massaged, you are free to use your hands and get on with life. But for those whose parenting style doesn't include carrying the baby regularly, for various reasons, massage might be a lovely way to give the baby the touch of skin and firm pressure that she craves.

Dummies

Many families find a pacifier useful as they patch together strategies that meet the baby's sensory needs. As we've seen, babies love to suck. Some health professionals have been anxious about reliance upon pacifiers, because when a breastfed baby is sucking on a dummy, the milk supply is not being stimulated. In fact, the research would suggest that pacifier use doesn't undermine breastfeeding. I'd still be inclined to wait, though, until you're happy that any underlying breastfeeding problems have been sorted out before you try it.

WRAPPING

Wrapping is another popular strategy, but the evidence that wrapping makes babies more settled is not convincing, and I've never particularly recommended it. Wrapping isn't safe if the baby is in your bed, or once the baby can turn over. Unfortunately, wrapping babies so that their legs are held together and extended out flat on the mattress increases the risk of hip dysplasia, or hip dislocation. If you want to try wrapping your baby, make sure he is not overdressed, use a muslin or light cotton wrap, and make sure he can move his hips, legs and feet freely (which to my mind rather defeats the purpose!). I didn't wrap my babies because I wanted to keep my life simple. The times I tried it, I'd no sooner finished carefully cocooning them, when it became apparent they wanted a breastfeed – which meant unwrapping them again because babies need their hands free to feed. In the night, having to re-wrap or re-zip into a sleeping suit after a breastfeed can rouse the baby, and make return to sleep harder for everyone.

Stepping outdoors

In 1988, when I worked in Indigenous health, I slept for a week in a swag in a dry red-dirt gully on the Pitjantjatjara lands in Central Australia, and observed first-hand the parenting style that characterised the first months of an Aboriginal child's life in more traditional communities. The babies were never alone. They were either filling their tummies with breast milk, or bumping along on someone's hip, or nestled in someone else's lap, or tied to someone else's body. Their wide little black eyes feasted on the complex light and shading of the red sand country, the ten thousand shapes and colours of the gully, the spinifex and the desert oaks. Their skin knew the hot breeze, their ears knew the sounds of bird calls and rustling leaves mingling with human voices, their nostrils knew the smell of the camp fire and of sweat and of gumleaf crushed. The events of their world flooded every sensory organ with nourishment. I didn't hear those babies crying. People who lived or worked in more traditional Aboriginal communities in the 1980s and 1990s told me repeatedly that the babies didn't cry. Then they would add: 'And the breast is always in the baby's mouth.'

Even the most elaborate and expensive play-gym offers extremely limited visual or auditory stimulation, only momentarily satisfying a baby's hunger for sensation. In the crying period, a baby in a cot or on the floor is still not able to roll or crawl, and unable to create her own satisfying vestibular or touch or proprioceptive stimulation; the static four walls of a room close out the complex, constantly changing, deeply satisfying visual and auditory and olfactory and tactile sensory experiences of an outdoor environment.

Next time your baby is caught in a crying loop, try stepping outside the house. This will, of course, require consideration of the constraints of climate – though when the right precautions are taken, babies love to be out of the house regardless of the weather. Very often, parents find that stepping outside the home immediately settles the baby down, enough to try a feed, for instance, or enough for the baby to drop off to sleep. The changing colour, the breeze, the symphony of sounds, the feeling of the sky opening up, the change of temperature, the bigger world in its extraordinary richness, floods the baby's brain with sensation.

DOES BODYWORK HELP?

These days, many parents in developed countries take their crying babies to see manipulative therapists – mostly cranio-sacral therapists, osteopaths and chiropractors. These practitioners argue that birth disrupts structural alignment of the skull and spine, causing crying, and that breastfeeding problems result from tight fascia and muscles, and subtle misalignments.

However, as we have seen, crying problems resolve with the passage of time. The interventions of bodywork therapists for infant crying and breastfeeding problems certainly help parents to feel supported while the baby develops and grows out of the problem, but research does not show any other significant benefit of bodywork therapies for crying babies. That's not to say that osteopathic interventions aren't useful for musculoskeletal problems in adults. (I have regularly referred patients to see osteopaths, beginning in the 1980s, long before osteopathy and musculoskeletal medicine became more mainstream.)

It makes sense that babies delivered with the help of vacuum extraction or forceps might have headaches, painful bruising or swelling which sets feeds off to a bad start. It's understandable that in a society where clinical breastfeeding support is so poorly understood, caring manipulative therapists, with their sensitivity to oral and cranial function, are stepping into the gap to try and help. But the theory that impingement on the nerves of the head and neck (that is neither medically significant nor detectable) results in subtle tongue dysfunction, doesn't make sense in the context of the many other more direct explanations for breastfeeding problems and what we now know about the biomechanics of suckling.

I don't believe that subtle asymmetries need 'fixing' for breastfeeding to succeed, since good healthy function itself reinforces healthy structural alignment. You might be interested in experimenting with the holistic gestalt approach to breastfeeding, which helps your baby relax and enjoy the repeated experience of healthy oromotor function and protective spinal alignment, many times a day. I think of the gestalt method as a powerful and empowering form of bodywork. Finding good clinical breastfeeding help is important if a breastfed baby cries a lot, and sometimes, if the breastfeeding problems are minor and we've done all we can, we just need to continue experimenting, and allow the baby time to practise.

Pam: 'He seemed to need to feel the world pushing back in against him.'

From birth, my son Tommy's physicality was noticeably different to his older sister's. He was prone to much more vigorous movement of his little limbs than Emma had been, with more flailing around and unsettled behaviours. He seemed to need to feel the world pushing back in against him. His father was unavailable much of the time, and I tried to contain Tom against my body whenever I could, in a carrier or in my arms, though of course I couldn't always do so since there were other needs to attend to, including my own. I worked two or three mornings a week in general practice from when both my babies were 6 weeks old, and when I worked, the children were cared for by friends or went into family day care.

I tried to have the three of us outdoors as often as possible to escalate Tommy's doses of healthy sensory nourishment, which was easy to do in the Blue Mountains where we lived. I'd walk to the shops with them in a stroller that fitted them both. We also led a busy social life with other women in the neighbourhood who had very young children. Tommy was lucky to have his sister Emma bouncing about in perpetual motion when we were inside the house, giving him rough hugs, sloppy kisses and generally making a happy (or sometimes not so happy) racket. He found her endlessly entertaining.

My little son didn't end up being a baby who screamed for long periods, so I was blessed. But he was still hard work, and the days were utterly exhausting. Yet what I remember now, when I think back, is just how much delight and laughter there was for me in both Emma and Tommy's early lives, in the midst of my fatigue. I'm grateful that I had the opportunity to prioritise both my own social needs and a very physical relationship with my babies at such a vulnerable time.

7

A GOOD (ENOUGH) NIGHT'S SLEEP

For many new families, life revolves around sleep. Mothers and fathers are told that 'sleep breeds sleep', so they spend hours trying to get their babies to sleep during the day in the hope that they will wake less at night.

You know the story. You've put her down for a nap in her cot and she begins to grizzle. You've been told to leave her as long as you can so that she learns to 'self-settle' but she soon works herself up to a full-blown cry – long, shuddering wails that sound as if she has been abandoned on the frozen ground with wolves looming in the shadows, not placed in a safe little cot by a devoted mother. You try patting, but she screams on. Finally you can't bear it anymore and you reach in and pick her up. Her breath catches with sobs as her crying quietens. She bobs her head against you as if to feed, but surely she can't be hungry, you think to yourself. She had a big feed before you put her down and you've been told not to over-feed her. So you rock her gently until she falls asleep, still shuddering with those little sobbing hiccoughs. You breathe her in, stroking her little downy scalp, kissing the tip of her ears until the funny jerky little movements of her eyes under the lids have finished, until her little breaths are slow and steady. Carefully, carefully, so as not to disturb her, you lay her down.

And just as you tiptoe out the bedroom door, she flails suddenly, with a piercing shriek, and begins to scream again.

Hannah: 'I've let him set up bad habits and now I'm paying for it.'

Hannah sits down, and looks at 4-month-old Ben sleeping in the pram.

'It's unusual that he's sleeping,' she says in an unsteady voice. 'He never does that.' And then she begins to cry.

I move the tissues a little closer. Hannah takes one and presses it carefully against each eye, dabbing up the tears, trying not to smudge the eyeliner.

'I've got to do something,' she says, 'I really have. I can't go on like this. My husband is worried about me. He thinks we should do controlled comforting.'

'How often does he wake?' I ask.

'Six or seven times at night,' she says. 'I put him in the cot at 6.30 p.m. and he'll wake up three or more times throughout the evening. I can't relax with my husband because at any moment I'm expecting Ben to cry. Then from 10 o'clock, when we go to bed, he may go for a few hours straight – that's his best sleep of the day. After about two in the morning he wakes every hour or so.'

Hannah says she tries to pat Ben back to sleep during the night, and that works sometimes. But if he starts crying in earnest she feeds him, which always works. Then Hannah lies there, wide awake, dreading the next time, strung tight as a wire.

Hannah's sleep consultant told her that Ben was overtired and overstimulated and that she needed to get him into a daytime sleep routine if she wanted better nights. The nurse told her to watch him for signs of tiredness, and to put him in the cot with the blinds down as soon as she saw them, before he got too upset.

'But the minute I put him in the cot he starts to grizzle.'

The sleep consultant also told Hannah that Ben needs to be given space to learn to self-settle, and that she is supposed to leave the bedroom. When Ben was younger Hannah would do 'responsive settling' – waiting until he'd had three or four big cries before going back in and patting him to sleep. She'd pat and pat and pat (sometimes for three-quarters of an hour!) and even sneak in a feed sometimes. Now, she's been told to wait for as long as she can before going in.

'It's so hard. No matter how long I wait, he just seems to keep on screaming. Once I let him cry for 40 minutes. It was horrible. In the end I had to go back in and pick him up. I feel like a terrible mother for letting him get so distressed and upset. Then I feel like a terrible mother for being so weak-willed because I can't let him cry for longer, even though I know it's best for him in the long-run.' Fresh tears slide down her cheeks. 'I don't know what to do.'

Hannah believes Ben is crying because he is desperately overtired – he cries each time he wakes up during the day and won't sleep for more than 20 or 30 minutes, no matter what she tries.

'It's my fault,' she tells me from the chair. 'At mothers' group I can't say anything. It's too humiliating. Their babies are all sleeping through the night.'

Even when Ben is awake, Hannah is reluctant to leave the house. She is too exhausted, shattered. She constantly watches the clock, marking the time that has to pass before the next sleep is due. She watches Ben for tired cues, hoping that he will be soon ready for a nap. Hannah's brain is an aching fog, a ravenous yearning for sleep, day after tedious day.

Her love for her baby is visceral, gut-wrenching, complete. She loves Ben more than she had ever imagined possible, and yet he is her tormenter, her prison. It is only when his small lids close that Hannah feels free.

How has this happened?

UNDERSTANDING THE BIOLOGY OF SLEEP

Although most healthy, happy babies wake and signal for their parents in the night in the first year of life, I have observed that parents' night-time sleep is also *unnecessarily* disrupted in our society. This is because we place obstacles in the way of the biological processes that regulate healthy sleep, in both babies and their parents. There is a great deal of unnecessary daytime sleep distress, too, because of the mistaken belief that 'sleep breeds sleep' – that the more a baby sleeps during the day, the better her night-time sleep.

A baby's sleep, like our own, is regulated by the alignment of two unconscious biological processes: sleep/wake homeostasis and the circadian clock. We cannot make our baby, or ourselves, sleep – we can only remove the obstacles that interfere with the healthy function of these two regulators and their alignment.

Sleep pressure

In both adults and babies, sleep pressure (the internal feeling of 'sleepiness') builds with each passing hour of wakefulness, and dissipates when we go to sleep. The regulator of sleep pressure is known as the sleep/wake homeostat, and is mediated by the build-up and then dissipation of particular chemicals in the brain. The sleep/wake homeostat also regulates how deeply we sleep in response to how much sleep we've had in the preceding hours or days. The less sleep we've had, the deeper (and longer) we sleep, to compensate.

In babies fresh out of the womb, sleep pressure rises very quickly and they are often only awake for short periods.

As adults, we generally manage to get through the day without feeling overcome by the growing sleep pressure. Sleep pressure becomes very pronounced in the mid- to late evening, though, until we are so sleepy that we have to go to bed. In both babies and adults, the function of a daytime nap is to take the edge off the building sleep pressure, so that we can comfortably last until bedtime.

The circadian clock

The circadian clock is a cluster of 50,000 cells buried deep in the brain. It regulates the various bodily functions which cycle over roughly a 24-hour period. Daily resetting of this circadian clock is necessary to keep it exactly aligned with the 24-hour day, and light falling on the retina in the eye is a powerful environmental cue for this calibration.

The circadian clock releases what's known as an alerting signal, which travels up from the brain stem and hypothalamus to keep the cerebral cortex alert and aroused. This alerting signal builds in strength over the course of a day, perhaps ebbing briefly in the early afternoon when even adults in many cultures like to take a nap.

Newborns are not long out of the womb's deep darkness and not yet attuned to the sun's rhythms so, at first, their quickly building sleep pressure is the dominant regulator of their sleep, which may not necessarily coordinate with our real time of day and night. But as the days and weeks progress, daylight programs the brain and the circadian clock matures. Soon, most of a baby's sleep occurs at night-time.

Daylight, however, is not the only environmental cue that helps to set the baby's circadian clock to align with day and night. Babies also need the activities of daily living to help calibrate their circadian clocks: conversation, footsteps, siblings' noisy play, clanging of cooking utensils, taps running, toilets flushing, cupboard doors banging, caresses and interactions. Exposure to these environmental cues mature the circadian clock more rapidly from the very first days of life, and this is one reason why it's best to have the baby sleeping in the same room as the caregiver, even during daytime naps. The other reason is that having the baby sleeping in the same room as the caregiver day or night, always on her back, protects against sudden infant death syndrome.

Alignment of sleep pressure and the circadian clock

The sleep/wake homeostat and the circadian clock need to align for easy, healthy sleep. In adults, the circadian clock's alerting signal acts to counteract the building sleep pressure as the day progresses, and is at its most powerful in early evening when the sleep pressure is very strong. As soon as the circadian clock's alerting signal begins to ebb, sleep pressure takes over, and we are overwhelmed by tiredness. During a night's sleep, as sleep pressure dissipates, the circadian clock not only ceases emitting its alerting signal, but sends messages that actively turn off cerebral cortex arousal. This is why, even as the sleep pressure disappears, we continue to sleep. In the morning, when the circadian clock starts to send out an alerting signal again (and there is no more sleep pressure), we awaken.

EVERY BABY IS DIFFERENT

Although sleep pressure and the circadian clock are the two most powerful forces shaping your baby's sleep, every baby is unique and your baby's sleep needs will depend partly on her developmental maturity at birth (which varies significantly between normal babies) and partly on her genetic predisposition.

The difference between infants who sleep the most and those who sleep the least is greatest at birth, but remains remarkably large at 6 months and beyond. A newborn may sleep for a total of 9–20 hours a day, and the *whole range* is normal. By 6 months of age, babies can sleep anywhere from just less than 9 hours up to 17 hours a day. This means your baby may sleep half as much as the baby next door in a 24-hour period, and yet both babies are completely normal!

Individual babies also show wide variations in sleep from one day to another with, astonishingly, a difference of up to 12 hours between different days in the one baby, according to one study. That is, like us, babies might have a day when they sleep less, and then they catch up the following day because of sleep/wake homeostasis. This balancing over time is normal, and doesn't mean that the baby will be fussy. Similarly, because babies' circadian clocks mature at different rates, some have up to four regular daytime sleeps throughout their first 6 months, others just one; for many, daytime sleep is brief and irregular. Once feeding problems are sorted out, it's quite normal for babies to only catnap during the day. Whatever the length and number of daytime naps your baby takes, if it's working for you, consider it normal.

YOU DON'T HAVE TO 'TEACH' YOUR BABY TO SLEEP

Various factors, such as whether the baby is fed breast milk or formula, where the baby sleeps, and how quickly parents respond to the baby's cries, interact with the biological regulation of sleep. These effects have to be kept in perspective, however, because they only very modestly influence the fundamental and hardwired biological make-up of each baby's sleep.

Many parents are given the impression that it's their responsibility to teach babies to sleep, and that their parenting style or whether or not they are breastfeeding may have caused sleep problems. They might also feel that if they don't *do* something, they will allow bad sleep habits to take root, which will affect the child as the years pass and be bad for the child's development. None of this is true. In fact, if parents simply remove any obstacles to healthy sleep, and then proceed to enjoy the day, the baby's sleep will look after itself with minimal effort on your part.

You may have been told that you need to teach your baby to self-settle – that is, to put himself back to sleep without your help when he wakes up in the night. Actually, if we look at studies of thousands of normal babies, we see that the capacity to self-settle is innate, and develops with maturity over the first 2 years of life. Almost no newborns, and just over a third of babies at 3 months of age, sleep from 10 p.m. to 6 a.m. without disturbing their parents most (though not all) nights in the week. By 6 months, this number has grown to half of normal babies; the other half will always wake during the night. By 12 months, nearly three-quarters of babies sleep through most (though certainly not all) nights. Regular night-waking, and the inevitable maturation to self-settling over the first year or two, are biologically normal processes. Regular night-waking in the first year of life is not related to any long-term sleeping problems in children.

Attempting to intervene in the first 6 months (and even, the evidence shows, in the first year) with strategies to promote longer periods of uninterrupted sleep do not in fact have any beneficial effect on sleep or development later in childhood.

THE EXPECTATION OF UNBROKEN SLEEP

In the past century we've developed a belief in the West that a solid 7 or 8 hours of sleep (sometimes referred to as the 'die' model of sleep, or 'the night of the living dead'!) is both normal and necessary for our health. But all humans wake up intermittently throughout the night and are sensitive to what is happening in the environment, even if we don't remember it.

From the dawn of time and still in nomadic and hunter-gatherer cultures, humans got up in the night to kindle the fire for instance, or to check the weather or the animals, or to respond to worrying signs of predators. Or we woke up and shared important thoughts with our fellow sleepers. Normal 'sleep architecture' (the way we cycle through quiet and deep sleep) is modified by many different factors, including having a partner or baby or sibling sleeping nearby, or by how much sleep we've had over the past few days, or by the time of night. The word 'architecture', with its connotations of solid structures, is misleading because sleep architecture in healthy normal infants and adults is fluid and changeable, adaptable both within the one night, and from night to night.

Some historians argue that two-phase or segmented sleep was usual in the West up until the industrial revolution. Hundreds of literary references refer to the 'first' and the 'second' sleeps. People lay down and went to sleep for a number of hours once the working day was over and dinner shared. It was too hard to keep sleep at bay when night reached in to surround and swallow the vulnerable, flickering flame. But then they woke up for an hour or two in the middle of the night. They had sex or got up to attend to a few things, or, once literacy was more widespread, read by candlelight and reflected, before going back to sleep for another few hours until daylight. Segmented sleep appeared to remain quite common even until the late 1800s, when oil lamps and candles were finally replaced by the coal-powered innovations of kerosene and gas lights. The cheap availability of good light at night soon allowed for social interactions and cinema and theatre and reading until late, at least in the cities, and therefore created the need to compress sleep into one long block. This was a major social shift.

Now, throughout the world, the electric light bulb has thoroughly displaced sprawling, segmented sleep. Nevertheless, an unbroken night's sleep is still not typical of many adults' sleep pattern in the West, despite our expectations, and may not be expected in more traditional cultures.

In fact, a close look at the evidence shows that it is not the number of times a mother is woken by her baby that is linked with an increased risk of depressed and anxious mood, but how long it takes her to go back to sleep once she is woken – that is, what we call her 'sleep efficiency'. And that's good news, because there are a number of strategies that have been proven to help with sleep efficiency, which we will explore in the next chapter.

REMOVING THE OBSTACLES TO HEALTHY BABY-SLEEP

We don't get anxious about whether or not our cat is taking enough sleep. We shove her off our laps, nudge her off our favourite chair, we wake her up mercilessly and she curls up and purrs back to sleep. We trust the cat will take the sleep that she needs one way or another. If the cat is grumpy, we don't think, *Quick! I have to get the cat to sleep!* We realise, if we think about it at all, that there might be all sorts of explanations for the cat's grumpiness. We trust that if she needs sleep badly enough, she'll lie down and go to sleep. We trust in the integrity of our cat's biological sleep regulators.

Similarly, we don't have to teach our babies to sleep, or to count up the hours. We can't *make* babies sleep. But we can trust our baby's biological competence, we can trust that babies will take all the sleep they need, as long as we remove the obstacles that get in the way of healthy sleep regulation.

The two biological factors which most commonly disrupt a baby's sleep in the first few months of life are (not surprisingly!) the hunger for milk, and the hunger for sensation. This is because each kind of hunger results in high levels of sympathetic nervous system arousal, which override the chemical effects of the building sleep pressure.

Satisfying your baby's hunger for milk

In babies, milk in the belly and the experience of nestling into the carer's body switch on hormones of satiety, relaxation and trust and build into a wave of sleepiness known as postprandial somnolence. If the baby's sleep pressure is also rising, the combination of postprandial somnolence and sleep pressure becomes a very powerful biological trigger for sleep in babies. Adults, too, may experience vestiges of postprandial somnolence after a satisfying meal. But in babies, falling asleep when the tummy is full is a powerful and hardwired biological event, quite difficult to disrupt.

As the baby slips into sleep, her little eyes move rapidly and irregularly under those translucent lids, in what's known as dreaming or active or rapid-eye-movement (REM) sleep. Her small limbs jerk slightly and shudder and her breath may be a little irregular and rapid. After 10 or 20 minutes of this light sleep, she may settle down into a deep, non-REM sleep (quiet sleep), with floppy limbs and slow regular breaths. In quiet sleep, the baby is much harder to rouse.

Newborns slip between periods of active and quiet sleep quickly, and the boundary between active and quiet sleep may be quite blurred. By observing her cues, you will quickly work out that once your baby falls from active sleep into quiet sleep, she is less likely to stir if you put her away from your body. If she wakes without falling into quiet sleep, that's of no concern: the sleep/wake homeostat will ensure that she has enough quiet sleep later on. A full sleep cycle, if it happens, might take about 45 minutes, although this is variable. There is no need for me to show you graphs: you need only watch your baby.

Does formula help babies sleep?

From about 3 months of age, breastfeeding babies tend to wake and disturb their parents more often in the night compared to formula-fed babies. However, the evidence shows that breastfeeding mothers have the same sleep durations overall.

The increased number of times breastfeeding babies wake their parents at night after 12 weeks of age also needs to be held in perspective. Up until 8 weeks of age, the *upper* end of the normal range of times babies disturb their parents over

8 hours, whether they are fed breast milk or formula or both, is three and a half times (roughly every 1½–2 hours), and this drops to three times for babies 3–6 months. So the *average* number of times of night-waking is substantially less than that.

If the baby is consistently waking more often than the upper end of the normal range, let's say as often as hourly during the night, I would expect to find an underlying problem, such as an unidentified feeding issue, misalignment of the two sleep regulators, or viral infection.

Breastfeeding mothers tend to go back to sleep more easily in the night – that is, they have better sleep efficiency. This may be due to the effects of high prolactin levels at night, and the oxytocin surge of the feed, or it may be due to the fact that it's more disruptive for formula-feeding mums to have to get out of bed and make up a bottle. Once formula-fed babies are awake at night, they also have a tendency to stay awake for longer periods. However, parents who are formula-feeding can still aim to replicate the sleep-inducing hormonal effects of the feeding system of the breast, with low lighting, skin contact, cuddles and caresses.

Satisfying your baby's hunger for sensation
As we've discussed, parents are often told that babies become overtired because they are overstimulated, and that they should strip the cot of distracting, stimulating colour and pictures and toys. But a baby placed down in the cot often cries because of the absence of interesting or comforting sensation, and some babies are conditioned into associating the cot with miserable feelings of loneliness or boredom, making it even harder for the biological sleep regulators to do their job.

A baby's longing for rich sensation in the night is biologically hardwired, though influenced by temperament or genetics. This is why the safest place to sleep your baby is in the same room: the sharing of sensory information between the caregiver and the baby, which often occurs unconsciously – the sound of each other's breathing, the little stirrings and murmurs – protects the baby. The longing for sensory nourishment in the night translates into a need for physical contact with the parent.

Protecting the circadian clock

In addition to the disruptive effects of the hunger for milk or sensation, a baby wakes more often during the night when his sleep/wake homeostat and circadian clock are prevented from getting in sync. This commonly occurs during the crying period and indeed throughout the first year of life as an unintended side-effect of strategies that aim to accelerate self-settling. That is, unnecessarily long sleeps during the day often, after a few weeks, results in excessive night-waking.

This effect is most marked in babies who have lower sleep needs. The sleep/wake homeostat's alignment with the circadian clock is disrupted by the long daytime sleeps, so that it may be only very late at night before the felt sleep pressure builds enough to override the alerting signal of the circadian clock. Or the baby may go to sleep early in the evening, but begins to wake frequently from the small hours of the morning because the sleep pressure has dissipated and the rhythm of the circadian clock's alerting signals has been disrupted.

Deliberate exposure to environmental cues (those that signal daytime during the day and those that signal night-time during the night) keeps the alignment of the sleep regulators healthy.

Hannah (Part 2): 'Why didn't someone tell me this sooner?'

I check Ben over, and he is perfectly healthy. Hannah and I begin to talk.

'Little Ben might only need half as much sleep as another baby, believe it or not,' I explain, 'so only you can know how much sleep he needs during the day. If you try to put him to sleep but find he won't drop off, then really, the best thing for you to do is to get on with your day and forget about trying to make him sleep.'

Hannah looks at me as if I'm crazy. 'But then he'll be *seriously* overtired and it will be even worse!' she says

'Why don't you try it for a week and see?' I suggest.

She looks at me doubtfully.

'You'll also need to help his sleep regulators,' I continue. I give her a brief explanation about sleep pressure and a baby's circadian clock. 'I suspect that all that time in a darkened room during the day means his sleep regulators are not well aligned with day and night at the moment.'

'That's so interesting!' Hannah says. 'No-one ever tells you that!'

'So the first step to keeping the circadian clock healthy is to get up at about the same time each day. I know it's so tempting to sleep in if we can – and to persuade Ben to sleep in, too, after a ragged night – but this just perpetuates the problem. It's not that you have to actively wake him, though some parents decide to do that. You could decide the time *you'll* get up every morning, then pull back the curtains, let the sunlight spill in, start making the usual noises. Soon he'll detect these cues, even if he's asleep, and start to sync his clock with yours and with real time.'

'That makes sense,' Hannah says. 'I can try that.'

'Okay, then my next suggestion would be to try to get as much daylight early in the morning for you both. Since physical activity also helps set your circadian clock, and is terrific for everyone's mood, you could do something like start the day with a walk, or even just put him outside on a rug while you hang out the clothes or something.'

Hannah's eyes are lighting up. It turns out she loves her garden, and it's been sorely neglected.

'I always thought it would be too cold to go out in the morning,' she says.

'But babies love the outdoors, and as long as you rug him up when it's cold, it would be good for you both!' I say. 'And then for the rest of the day the most important thing is that you continue to get out and do the things you like doing.'

Hannah nods, but I can tell she is feeling uncertain again. 'But everyone tells me he needs to be *less* stimulated, that he's been so unsettled because he's overstimulated.'

'I understand what you're saying, and you are the one who knows your baby better than anyone. But things seem to be awful for you at the moment, so maybe you could experiment with something new, to see what you think?'

Ben stirs in the pram, and Hannah starts to rock it a little.

She's considering my suggestion.

'You could also experiment with putting him to bed later at night. Did you know that many babies around the world don't settle until about 9 or 9.30 p.m.?'

'Oh!' she exclaims. 'But the evening is the only time I get with my husband.'

'Yes, that's important, I know. The reason I'm suggesting this is that if you put him to bed closer to your own bedtime, Ben's best night-time sleep is more likely to coincide with yours.'

'Well my husband *does* complain that he never gets to see Ben because I put him to bed at around the time he gets home,' she concedes.

'Could he take the baby for a play or a walk and give you a break when he comes in?'

'Maybe. Or maybe I'd rather that we just all be together,' she says.

'That's a brilliant suggestion!' I respond. 'Sharing time with Ben in the evenings could be lovely for all of you! It's weighing up the pros and cons, isn't it, and by introducing gradually later bedtimes and a regular get-up time over the next couple of weeks, we'd expect the excessively frequent waking from 2 a.m. to decrease.'

Ben is still fretting, and Hannah lifts him out of the pram. 'Normally I'd think that I just have to wait until he goes to sleep and let him grizzle,' she says.

'I know this is not what you are used to hearing, but if he wants to sleep, he will, as long as he has had enough to drink and enough cuddles and sensory stimulation.'

Ben is now sitting on Hannah's lap, and Hannah is holding

a little blue terry-towelling octopus in front of her. Ben gurgles happily. We both smile.

'One more thing,' I say. 'At nights, you could make sure you respond in a relaxed and lazy way, with dimmed lights. If we're anxious and jumping to every sound, it tells the baby there's something to worry about. You might try soothing words, a few little pats before offering a feed, but remember: your overall aim is to keep him and yourself as relaxed and drowsy as you can and to get in with a feed before there is any serious revving up. Don't burp him, or do anything that wakes him up. Avoid nappy changes if you can.'

Hannah leaves feeling hopeful. When she comes back in a week's time, she sits down, takes Ben out of the pram and looks hard at me.

'I just cannot believe how much easier it's been. Why didn't someone tell me this sooner?'

DELIBERATELY DELAYING RESPONSES DOESN'T HELP

Sometimes, strategies that aim to accelerate self-settling or make babies sleep for longer periods at night leave a painful legacy, because they make it difficult for parents to trust their baby's communications, and to trust themselves to respond appropriately.

The strategy of 'controlled crying' – letting the child cry himself to sleep in a separate room – is no longer recommended in any age group. Even the strategy of 'controlled comforting', where parents are advised not to let baby cry alone indefinitely, but to go in and out of the baby's separate room to pat and comfort, without picking him up – is largely out of fashion now for babies under 6 months, as the benefits of cued care and sleeping in the same room have become widely appreciated. There's still a chance that you've been told to respond to a baby who is calling out in the night (particularly after 3 months) by staying with him and sitting beside the cot, patting the mattress or patting the baby – but not by picking him up. However, since most health professionals now recognise the importance of responding with night feeds in the first 6 months, today's parents are more likely to be advised to tolerate some grizzling, or a few big cries, or a longer period of crying, before responding with a feed when the baby signals in the night. That is, you're advised that it's best to help your baby into good habits by delaying responses to his cues, perhaps from birth, perhaps from 6 weeks, perhaps from 3 months. You may have been told that this approach is consistent with 'cue-based care', and is a healthy form of limit setting. But this approach doesn't comprise cued care in the way that I define the term.

It's not cued care because you are still asked to *deliberately delay your responses* to what you know the baby wants (that is, to be picked up or fed), or *to not respond at all* to what you know the baby wants (that is, to be picked up or fed), even though you might make other responses. The beliefs underlying the strategy of delayed responses are that teaching the baby not to expect to be picked up or fed gradually extinguishes the crying-out behaviour in the night, and that an increase in the amount of unbroken sleep you get at night must surely benefit you, the baby, and the family.

Yet for babies in the first year of life, these beliefs are not supported by the evidence. Sleep training approaches have not been shown to decrease night-waking in the first year of life. Also, it's *not the number of times of waking* that cause mothers to feel miserable: it's being awake for a long time, or regularly taking a long time to get back to sleep (that is, poor sleep efficiency) that causes distress. (However, if the baby's sleep pattern is seriously disrupted and the baby is waking excessively, that is, much more frequently than every couple of hours, then I would suggest that you turn to the Possums Baby and Toddler Sleep Program or an NDC accredited practitioner for help. More details about both of these can be found in the resources section.) Moreover, as you'd expect, the evidence confirms that delaying responses results in more crying and fussing in babies overall. Certainly the modest increase in uninterrupted sleep has not been shown to help a mother's mental health (though the support of any caring health professional helps her mental health, regardless of the program). And the research definitely shows that attempting to change the baby's sleep biology with sleep training in the first 6 months of life does not improve the baby's sleep habits or development down the track.

The greatest concern, to my mind, is that deliberately delaying responses to your baby's cues risks serious communication confusion between yourself and the baby. Over the years, I've watched the confidence of parents plummet as well-meaning health professionals give detailed instructions on the meaning of, and how and when parents should respond to, their baby's cues.

You are the expert on your baby. You are uniquely

positioned to experiment, and to learn the meaning of your own baby's patterns of communications over time. Once the underlying problems that this book discusses are properly addressed, responding sensibly to a baby's cues makes life (and sleep) easiest for families, now and later.

'FEED-PLAY-SLEEP' CYCLES MESS WITH YOUR BABY'S SLEEP BIOLOGY

'Feed-play-sleep' cycles are also widely recommended in the belief that if we can teach babies to go back to sleep in the cot without a feed or physical contact, life would be more manageable for the family. This means teaching babies not to associate sleep with feeds or with being held *during the day* as well as at night. As a result, parents all around the developed world have been told to ignore the powerful biological cue of sleepiness at the end of a feed.

Burping, with its vigorous patting, upright position, and pressure on the tummy, is one way babies are kept awake after feeds. Some mothers tell me they even try to keep the baby awake after he falls asleep feeding during the night – whether by burping, changing the nappy, or walking around the house talking and interacting until the baby is alert – in order to lay him down in the cot awake, as instructed. It's not surprising that the baby then cries and takes a long time to go to sleep. And it's not surprising that it takes parents ages to relax after that and get back to sleep themselves.

During the day, once the baby has been stimulated enough to override the powerful, biologically driven sleepiness after a feed, it's then 'play-time', when you are supposed to interact with your baby, or put the baby on the floor with a mobile or toys. But true play is spontaneous and unstructured! That's why it's fun – there's no effort or planning involved. It's so much easier if interaction and enjoyment of each other simply suffuses the days as you go about your life, baby by your side. You don't schedule this play; it comes upon you in little moments. Watch that baby's tiny face! She is so ravenously hungry for your attention, your touch; she gazes into your eyes and mirrors your expressions and tries to talk back to you if you pause a moment, if you are willing to relax and take opportunities in the midst of the day's events to savour sensation, laughter, pleasure. The baby is utterly and exquisitely present to you, every feeling that crosses that darling little face transparent to you! The idea that the competent mother must structure the days hydraulically, with machine-like and predictable routines, arises directly out of last century's scientific paradigms. Twenty-first century scientific models embrace complexity – the idea that systems are made up of many dynamic and fluid interactions between parts – and aim to work *with* powerful biological forces, not against them.

Since the feed–play–sleep cycle affects every feed and every sleep (the most fundamental and repeated events in a new human's life), a family's daily life is comprehensively defined by this modern quest for self-settling. Dissociating sleep from feeds leaves parents rudderless, because the most dominant and repeated cue that the baby is ready to sleep has just fallen out of each day. If overtiredness does occur in the Western baby, it is because the basic biological cues of sleepiness are being repeatedly overridden.

SLEEP ALGORITHMS AND LISTS OF TIRED CUES ARE STRESSFUL AND CONFUSING

Since parents, in the quest for self-settling, are asked to ignore the fundamental biological cue of sleepiness that arises naturally with a feed many times a day, how then can they be expected to know *when* to put their baby down in the cot to sleep? To solve this problem, two strategies have been employed: sleep algorithms and lists of tired cues.

Sleep algorithms

Along with the feed-play-sleep routines, parents are given clock-based estimates indicating how long they can expect the baby to be awake for, and how long the baby should sleep. These algorithms are adjusted to the baby's age and may be very rigid, although these days they are more likely to be moderated by the disclaimer that 'all babies are different and this is a guide only'. Regardless, these sleep estimates cause a great deal of distress, because parents are asked to compare their child to averages which have little bearing on the highly variable needs of any individual baby.

Sleep algorithms also require parents to ignore, or at least minimise their response to, a second potent cue, the baby's pre-cry or cry cues. If the baby is put into the cot and grizzles and complains, the mother is warned that this is overtiredness, and that the baby should be allowed the space to learn to self-settle. But as we have seen, very often this only makes life harder for both mother and baby, as a baby's grizzles and cries are often communicating a hunger for milk or sensation or both.

Lists of 'tired cues'

Once you are told to ignore your baby's natural sleepiness at the end of feeds, and to ignore her grizzles and cries if she is hungry for milk or sensation, it would not be at all surprising if you became more and more disoriented and lost confidence in your capacity to communicate with your baby! At this point, you might be given lists of 'tired cues'. Unfortunately, a great deal of confusion also occurs because of these prescriptive lists. For example, parents might be told that a tired baby will grizzle, pull at his ears, close his fists, flutter his eyelids, back-arch or look worried. But these behaviours could result from other experiences (not all of which require parental response) and they could also be communicating that the baby needs more sensory stimulation.

Left to their own devices, parents and caregivers learn to read cues by pattern recognition. Each baby's system of communication is unique, and meaningful only in the context of the events in her little world. You contextualise your baby's communications, and build up a picture over time, experimenting with your responses in a sensible way so that you keep your baby's nervous system in balance, with her stress levels low. Only you can be an expert on what's best for your baby.

Sue: 'Now I would definitely put her to sleep.'

Sue, a fashion designer, looks at her 10-week-old baby lying in the pram. 'She's tired now.'

'How can you tell?' I ask, leaning in. Sue leans in too, the cotton of her full-skirted floral retro dress rustling.

'The red eyes. The way she bunches up her fists.'

The baby looks fine to me, though maybe she is a little grumpy from having to lie so long in her pram when every cell in her brain longs for sensory exploration. She gurgles and smiles at us peering in. Then she yawns.

'Now I would definitely put her to sleep, because she just yawned,' says Sue. 'I'd wrap her and lay her down. What do you think?'

'I really believe you are the expert on your baby,' I say. 'But do you ever yawn sometimes during the day, without needing to immediately lie down and go to sleep? I know I do!'

Sue smiles, and nods.

'We all yawn at times during the day – when we're relaxed, when we're a touch sleepy, when we're bored. But that doesn't signal an instant need to hit the pillow.' Sue watches her baby, who is now gazing at the green felt frogs hanging from the pram cover.

'Did you make them?' I ask, pausing for a moment to take a frog in my fingers and turn it over. It is hand-stitched, exquisitely sewn.

Sue nods again. 'I did it all when I was pregnant. There's no time for any of that now.'

'You're so talented!' I exclaim then return my attention to the task at hand. 'Why don't you try an experiment? In a situation like this, you could try going down to the shops, or hanging out the washing with her on a blanket on the grass at your feet, or doing something interesting together, instead of putting her in the cot.'

'But won't she get overtired?'

I explain that the best thing to do is to get on with the day and wait for the baby's *patterns* of tiredness to emerge before we take any steps to respond. Chances are the baby will eventually drop off to sleep without much effort on our part, wherever she is, if she is satiated with milk and satiated with sensation, and her sleep pressure has built up enough.

Sue decides to give it a go.

When I see her for the baby's 12-week vaccination, Sue tells me that the advice I gave her really helped, and that the days have been much easier. 'I just haven't been worrying about her sleep in the same way,' she says. 'It's a great relief, actually.'

CATNAPPING IS NORMAL DURING THE DAY

If your baby wakes after 40 minutes or less, you may have been told to re-settle your baby into a 'second sleep cycle' to prevent overtiredness and unsettled behaviour because 'sleep breeds sleep'. But this is a misinterpretation of the observation that content babies, whose needs for milk and sensation are sated, slide into sleep easily. Orchestrating a second sleep cycle requires elaborate instructions, in graphs and numbers, all of which present a somewhat misleading picture of sleep architecture, which is in fact fluid and variable.

If the baby cries on waking, hungering for sensation or milk, you may have been told to interpret this as tiredness and the need for 'a second sleep cycle'. These instructions give the false impression that there is an average amount of sleep any baby needs to be happy, and that scientific knowledge of sleep architecture is more useful than simply reading your baby's cues. Worse, they might undermine your confidence because of the instructions to *ignore* your baby's cues.

The aphorism I like to use, that calm breeds calm, is much more accurate, supported by large bodies of evidence from research in psychological and neurological science. Contentment and relaxation allow the sleep regulators to do their job. We can't always respond immediately to our baby, but what matters is our intention, our pattern of responding over time, so that the baby learns to expect that her needs will be met, on the whole, when she communicates them. Once she has learnt that, she is freed up from anxiety, she's more able to learn, she's more able to act confidently and independently as she matures – and more able to relax into easy sleep.

Angie: 'You mean we don't have to teach babies to self-settle?'

I'm watching a video about teaching babies to self-settle. I see a photogenic Baby Whisperer with a mane of glossy brown hair tie an infra-red video camera in place above a cot. Then she draws the bedroom curtains against the daylight.

The mother, Angie, strips the area around the cot bare of mobiles and wall hangings and pictures, removing all colourful objects from the bedside table, so that stimulation is minimised. The Baby Whisperer then instructs Angie to avoid eye-contact when she puts the 15-week-old baby down in the cot, and to avoid communication and smiles. The Baby Whisperer has wrapped sheet panels around the sides of the cot, with two slits cut along one side. We see her squat down and put her hands through these slits, patting the baby or sometimes the mattress. Angie squats beside her, watching and learning – two grown women hiding from a baby, patting a mattress.

Soon they do a strange crouching walk out of the room, a waddle with bottoms up in the air and hands on the floor. This is so the baby won't see them leave. The baby lies at the base of the cavernous cot, on his back, tucked in tight under folded-down sheets, crying hard.

How strange this is! How can the well-intentioned, big-hearted Baby Whisperer imagine that the baby doesn't know they are there, or that they are leaving? Babies are very sensitive to breathing, movements, sounds, even when they are asleep. And babies are smart! This little boy knows his mum and someone else is patting the mattress, he knows when they leave the room!

'You don't go in,' the Baby Whisperer says to Angie outside the room. 'Or if you have to go in, pat and then come out again, counting for longer and longer intervals each time. Let the numbers help you be strong.'

Angie and the Baby Whisperer huddle around the infra-red video watching to see that the baby is alright. He continues to cry. But not for long, a voice-over assures us. Rituals are put in place, the baby learns to self-settle, and it's all documented on camera.

Coincidentally, Angie comes in to see me a month later.

'I really believed in what we did, and it really did help for the next 3 weeks. But we went interstate the weekend before last and the last 10 days have been hell.'

'That's such a shame,' I say. 'But unfortunately, the effects of sleep training are not particularly stable in the first year of life. They last a while, but then the sleep training often has to be repeated.'

'But I *can't* go through it again,' Angie says, with desperation in her voice. 'We can't afford to pay the Baby Whisperer to come out again, and on my own I just can't let him cry for long!'

'There is something you can do,' I say carefully. 'But it will probably feel scary. We've all got used to the idea that life with a baby has to be hard now so that it will be better for everyone later on. But it's just not true.'

I tell her that she can try abandoning scheduled attempts to put the baby to sleep during the day, and let the baby fall asleep at the breast or with a bottle-feed or in arms, without counting the number of naps, or timing the length.

Angie looks at me in disbelief. For her, both feeding and sleeping have always been determined by *something* o'clock. She thinks I'm crazy when I suggest she disturb the baby whenever she wants to go out. She's been thoroughly convinced that 'sleep breeds sleep', and that if she doesn't follow the rules, the baby will be more unsettled and life will be even tougher.

I gently point out that life is already so hard she can hardly stand it. 'Just give it a try and come and see me next week. If you're not happy, you can go back to what you've been doing.'

Angie takes a deep breath. 'Okay,' she says, dubiously. 'I'm not sure how I'm going to explain this to my husband.'

'Self-settling is hardwired into babies and happens with maturity, though every baby is different, and some do it faster than others.'

Angie is astonished. 'You mean we don't *have* to teach babies to self-settle? They will learn to self-settle at night if we *do nothing*?'

'Exactly. It just mightn't happen as quickly as we want, but sometimes our efforts to hurry up self-settling actually make everything more stressful for everyone, without any true benefit.'

SLEEPING SAFELY

From the time we evolved into humans, and still largely unchanged today in much of the world's population and two-thirds of the world's cultures, the usual way of sleeping with a baby has been in the same bed. This, it has to be acknowledged, is the default sleep system for human beings.

But when societal structures were upended with the European industrial revolution and hunger drove families off the land and into the teeming cities; when men and women raised their children in flea-ridden, one-room tenements with everyone huddled together against the cold on a single straw mattress, some women suffocated their babies in the night. They lacked contraception, their older children were starving, and infanticide became poverty's desperate underbelly. The priests who heard the mothers' anguished confessions in the cold stone cathedrals began to sermonise from the pulpit against sharing a bed with babies (since how could they preach that every family should have the means to feed its children?).

'Sharing a bed with your baby causes babies to die!' they exhorted.

By the turn of the 20th century, experts in infant care continued to admonish against bed-sharing with children, though by then, thanks to Dr Freud's theories, it was judged to be immoral due to the risk of accidental witness of sexual activity.

My mother tells me that when she brought me home from hospital in 1960, she put my bassinet by her bed, but was told by the child health nurse at her very first visit a few days later to move me into another room. Families were told to sleep babies in separate rooms as another way of encouraging 'independence'.

In the late 1980s, when I was a young doctor, we'd noticed that babies were more settled sleeping on their tummies, and we told parents that prone sleeping protected against vomiting and reflux. Then in 1991, just before Tommy was born, there was enough evidence to show that lying prone put babies at risk of SIDS, due to asphyxiation, and we reversed our advice. A small number of babies, it seems, are slow to develop their brain-stem serotonin systems and more vulnerable to respiratory gas imbalances. If they are sleeping on their tummy, or are in very deep quiet sleep, these vulnerable babies are less likely to rouse if their airway obstructs. Oxygen levels drop, and they tragically succumb. The 'back to sleep' campaign resulted in a dramatic decrease in the incidence of SIDS.

From the 1990s, it was easy to support the historically constructed belief that bed-sharing was dangerous by claiming that it *must* increase the risk of SIDS.

David: 'I watched them sleep.'

David leans forward, his crisp, rolled-up white shirt-sleeves resting on his designer jeans, his shaven skull shining a little in the fluorescent light. His partner is slightly reclined in my blue leather lounge-chair, their 3-week-old baby asleep in her lap. I inquire where the baby sleeps at night. They look at each other.

'Never with us,' they reply almost in unison.

Then David adds, hesitantly, 'There was just one time ...' He takes a deep breath. 'Genevieve was so tired. The baby had been screaming for two hours straight without a break, and at 3 o'clock in the morning they both fell asleep in the bed.' He holds her gaze for a moment.

'All I wanted was for Genny to sleep,' he says, turning to me. 'I knew having them share the bed was dangerous, so I pulled up a chair and sat there by the side of the bed and watched them sleep. At seven I finally had to wake them up so I could go to work.'

I am deeply touched by this story, by the protective gaze of the father, hour after hour through the dark of night, listening to the breathing of his beloved partner and baby in a lonely vigil of love, through the birdsongs of the dawn chorus in the backyard, through the first grey light of morning, through the sounds of the first cars driving down the street.

And I am sad that these responsible people have been taught that the parent's body is like a lethal weapon in the night. That he felt he couldn't just lie down there beside these two people that he loved more than life itself, and sleep with them in the quietness.

Bed-sharing is safe (if you do it right)

Despite the prevailing powerful social condemnations of bed-sharing, nearly half of Western parents bed-share at least some of the night in the baby's first 3 months. In the dark and blurry nights with a little baby, families do whatever works at any particular time, and this speaks to the adaptability and creativity human beings display in response to life challenges.

The father goes in to sleep with the toddler, who has woken up crying; the baby starts out in the cot and comes into the parental bed; the mother may go off into the spare room for a night so she is less likely to hear the baby and the father brings the baby in when necessary. Mattresses are put onto the floor and bedrooms look chaotic.

Why does this happen? Why do parents bring babies into the bed, despite feeling guilty that they are doing the wrong thing? Because the babies sleep better; because the mothers sleep better; because they like it; because it is easier.

In the last decade, having observed that families bed-share with their babies regardless of prevailing expert advice, some researchers began to look more closely at the evidence. Is bed-sharing, which occurs so commonly, *actually* dangerous?

The truth is that no matter where our babies sleep, there will be risk. Driving cars results in horrific accidents, life-long injury and brutal deaths, but we don't ask citizens to stop driving cars. Instead, we focus on risk minimisation. Unfortunately, the simplistic attempt to eliminate risk by banning bed-sharing has had unexpected outcomes. The number of infant deaths on couches, lounge-chairs and recliners has increased, due to gaps and squashy corners which kink infant airways when the carer drops off to sleep and the baby slides down into them. Babies have suffered fractured skulls, slipping from the lap of exhausted mothers who were told they had to sit up on the side of hospital beds to feed.

Research has found that sharing a sleep surface places the baby at risk of SIDS under specific circumstances:

- The baby is premature.
- The baby is formula-fed.
- There is bedding (doonas or pillows) that may cover the baby's face.
- The baby is swaddled.
- The baby is left alone on the bed.
- The surface is a sofa, beanbag, couch or lounge.
- There are other children or pets in the bed.
- An adult in the bed smokes cigarettes, drinks alcohol or takes sedating medication.
- An adult in the bed is an unusually heavy sleeper or has sleep apnoea.
- The mattress is very soft or sagging or has a lamb's wool cover.
- The baby is positioned between two adults.
- There is a gap between the mattress and the wall.

Now the maternity hospitals in my state of Queensland educate parents about bed-sharing safely, aiming to minimise the risk since it is not possible to completely eliminate risk in any sleeping situation.

Pam: 'I can't find her!'

Emma slept between her father and myself in our old-fashioned, Bob Dylan-inspired, queen-sized brass bed. One night, when she was barely 2 weeks old, I lost her in the night. I woke to little baby-sounds, as if she wanted to feed. I reached out to touch her, but the space between us was empty. I felt around the sheets in the darkness. No baby.

I threw the bedclothes back, fumbling for the bedside light switch. No baby.

'I can't find her!' I cried.

Her father jumped up in fright and felt around frantically, too, throwing off the sheets, chucking pillows on the floor. Suddenly he was on the pine floorboards on his hands and knees, looking under the bed.

Then I heard her again. There she was, little legs in the air, hanging head-down through the bars at the head of the bed in the gap between the mattress and the wall, the Aberdeen splint that she wore for her dislocatable hip lodged between the bars. She was making happy little gurgling sounds. Apparently, she liked being upside down.

That was how I learnt that newborn babies can crawl, even if they have a splint on. Now I know that crawling is one of the mammalian feeding reflexes – she was looking for me. That was how I learnt it's not safe to leave a gap between the bed and the wall. Oh, my baby! Surely I must have been a bad, bad mother to have placed my baby at such risk!

But we'd done a lot of things right. In hindsight, with the benefit of the evidence, though none of this was clarified at the time, I did a few things wrong. By far the biggest risk came about because I placed her on her tummy to sleep sometimes, which was the habit back then. And there was that gap, big enough for a newborn to slide through, between the bedhead and the wall. (Even a mattress up against the wall can leave a squashy gap that a small body might slide into, depending on the mattress, obstructing airways.) If I were to do it all over again, I would undo the bed frame, say goodbye to my Bob Dylan fantasies for a time, and put the mattress on the floor.

I'd place her on her back. If the room was too small to put the mattress away from the wall, I'd at least check out any potential gap, and fill it with towels.

Both my babies woke regularly in the night throughout the first year, though I'd resolved never to look at the clock or count up. Tommy woke the most often. His father and I did the strange night-time dance that parents do, changing arrangements and locations throughout the house from night to night, and within the one night. Then there was the difficult time when, as a divorced single mother, I was managing night-waking on my own. I usually slipped right back into sleep after I'd got up to them, and went to bed fairly early most nights. I worked part-time in general practice and cared for my patients. That is, I adapted. And yes, suddenly they were big kids sleeping through and that time in our lives was over, forever.

Sometimes, now that they are grown and gone, I look back on those tumultuous early months of child-raising, the struggles and the pleasures, and I am grateful that I shared a bed with each of my babies. It was such a fleeting time of life! I remember the milky scent of them as if it was yesterday, the way I caressed their downy heads, kissed their hot little faces and pudgy limbs, their utter trust and need for me, and I know in my heart that the strong physicality of our bond at the very beginning protected my children and me against the worst of the storms to come.

There are many ways to be a loving and physically engaged parent. You may choose not to bed-share for a variety of reasons; a bassinet or cot in the same room works just fine for many. Increasingly, some families use protective baby-pods in the bed; others adopt side-car configurations. Most families' sleeping arrangements vary throughout the night. Only you can say what is right in your own unique family's situation.

8

ENJOYING YOUR BABY

Almost all women, even those blessed with very settled babies, experience a great deal of worry after the birth of their little one, and this worry is normal.

For a start, it is natural to feel anxious when we are facing any new challenge, and a baby is a *very* big new challenge. Not only that, but evolution has hardwired a particularly acute kind of worry into a mother's brain for at least the first 3 months post-partum as a way of ensuring the baby's safety in environments much more threatening than ours in the developed world today. Some women also emerge from their pregnancy and birth experiences already feeling traumatised, after unexpected complications, for example, only to be confronted with a baby who screams.

As a new mother, our baby's cry pierces us. Our heart beats faster and our breathing quickens. Usually our blood pressure rises, too, and we might feel our milk let down. Fathers also experience strong physiological responses when their babies cry, though these tend not to be as prominent as a mother's. When we cannot settle a crying baby with a feed or a cuddle, we may start to feel desperate. Our own amygdala switches on, our sympathetic nervous system revs up involuntarily, anxious thoughts stream through our minds, frantic feelings churn in our bellies and rise up through our chests, our muscles tighten. And, floating above these feelings there's often a miasma of tiredness, the thick, choking haze of sleep deprivation.

What a shock it is, then, for parents to find they are caring for their brand-new child in a world where the right kinds of practical and emotional support can be very difficult to find, and where women, before they know it, are often isolated at home with their babies for long periods of time. No wonder that at least one in ten new mothers in the West report feeling overwhelmed by anxiety, and one in seven are diagnosed with postnatal depression.

It is often comforting to know that anxious feelings are a normal and hardwired biological change in response to our own baby's crying. Indeed, *not* feeling them may even be a cause for concern, as in the case of a mother who suffers severe depression. How normal it is, too, to wish that we didn't have to endure the intense physical discomfort of sleep deprivation!

PUTTING SLEEP IN PERSPECTIVE

Interestingly, 40 per cent of adults of any age will tell you, if asked, that they've had regular symptoms of insomnia over the previous month, whether it be difficulty falling asleep, waking frequently and finding it difficult to get back to sleep, waking up early, waking up feeling unrefreshed or a combination of all of these. Oddly enough, despite feeling that we don't get enough of it, we also tend to view sleep as expendable in a world hungry for time: we sacrifice sleep, bite by bite, to our productivity, to getting ahead. We get home later and later at the end of the day, and our unwind time blurs into sleep time. Does this sound familiar? Night after night we override the body's ancient longing to relax into sleep and rest, then we panic if we can't suddenly switch off our high levels of sympathetic nervous system activation when we want to, if we can't suddenly step outside the hyper-arousal of our busyness!

There's a belief that you need 8 hours of sleep a night to be healthy; that you'll be afflicted by poor concentration, depression, obesity, poor immunity and a shorter life if you don't have that amount. Yet adults, like babies, have highly variable sleep needs. A study of more than a million adults showed that those who averaged 6–7 hours' sleep had *greater* longevity than those who got eight hours or more! There is no evidence that the average 8-hour sleeper functions better than the average 6- or 7-hour sleeper. There are also large gaps between our estimation of how much sleep we've had, and how much we've actually had when someone measures it. The research shows that we:

- underestimate how much we've slept at night
- overestimate the effects of sleep deprivation on our capacity to function
- don't need as much sleep as we think we do
- are prone to the unrealistic belief that healthy sleep has to be solid and uninterrupted.

Those who self-report more sleep deprivation, regardless of how much they've slept, are more prone to depression. (By 'self-report' I mean that they tell researchers that they feel tired, rather than having their sleep measured in some way.) Early parenthood aside, there is a very large subjective component to how adults experience the effects of broken nights. Some of us function quite normally, and are reasonably unperturbed; others of us are devastated by the broken nights, despairing and panicked because we worry we will be an insomniac for the rest of our lives (which unfortunately becomes much more likely if we worry about it!). Effective programs for adult sleep problems not only address the way we think about sleep, but also ask people to change their behaviours. For example, people with sleep problems are advised to:

- be careful about caffeine use
- avoid bright tablet or laptop screens in the couple of hours before bedtime, due to their disrupting effects on melatonin and the circadian clock
- only go to bed when they feel tired
- get up after 20 minutes or so if they can't sleep and do something relaxing
- get up at the same time each morning.

Unfortunately, popular baby-sleep advice actually *promotes* the kinds of thoughts and behaviours that adult sleep researchers tell us create or worsen adult sleep problems. Parents are led to believe they've absolutely *got* to stop the baby waking if they want to stay sane! But a mother whose heart sinks each time the baby wakes in the night is less likely to slide easily back into sleep.

Worrying about how much sleep you're getting, and trying hard to get more sleep, makes you less likely to sleep easily, because the worry turns up the throttle on the sympathetic nervous system, which interferes with the healthy function of your biological sleep regulators. Poor sleep efficiency means we are so wound up that we regularly take half an hour or more to fall asleep again after waking to the baby, or are unable to drop off for a nap when the baby is sleeping during the day. It is the *worry* about sleep, the attention paid to it when you have a baby, not the lack of sleep itself, which leads to poor sleep efficiency and predisposes us to depression. Dread of sleep deprivation breeds sleep deprivation.

It is also difficult for a mother to read her baby's communications in the night when she's feeling anxious or angry about being woken *yet again*. Feeling frightened about the effects of being woken makes it difficult for her to decide just how far she can relaxedly allow the baby to make little wriggles and sounds and grizzles or try patting in the hope that he'll go back to sleep, before responding with a feed or closer physical contact.

The mistaken belief that 'sleep breeds sleep' also predisposes mothers to postnatal depression because they then:

- limit their daily social and physical activity so that they can focus on getting the baby to sleep during the day, which means they feel isolated and unsupported (social contact and exercise are powerful antidepressants)
- spend long periods during the day in dim rooms 'helping the baby self-settle', which means mothers as well as babies are exposed to less daylight (sunshine is good for mood and aligns everyone's circadian clocks).

FIGHTING DISTRESSED THOUGHTS AND FEELINGS MAKES THEM WORSE

To be human is to have a constant stream of words and images passing through our minds: stories and memories from the past, judgements and comparisons, imaginings and fears about the future. To be human is also to have feelings, urges and sensations – some pleasant, some painful – ebbing and flowing, surging and subsiding throughout our bodies like the weather.

For many parents, the combination of sleep deprivation and feeling concerned about an unsettled baby becomes overwhelming. The mind's stories paint unhappy pictures: 'I'm a failure' or 'I'm obviously not doing this right' or 'My baby isn't getting enough sleep and this is going to harm us both'. Psychologists call this 'negative self-talk'.

The fact is, we all have distressing stories about our own incompetence that play through our minds – certainly I do. As a modern person, you have no doubt breathed in from childhood the desire for self-improvement; you may feel in your bones a strange dissatisfaction with yourself, your body, your personality, your achievements; you may feel the hunger to be *better* and *more* that typifies our age. In the West we won't buy bananas with spots on the skin, or misshapen carrots; we want to expunge weakness and vulnerability. We want to be pristine.

Sometimes, challenging negative stories and replacing them with positive ones might help. This is a form of cognitive behavioural therapy (CBT), and many psychologists and psychiatrists offer a variation of this technique. Deliberately cultivating gratitude is another popular strategy that is worthwhile practising. For example, you might tell yourself:

- 'I may not feel terrific, but I still have good days and I love my baby. I will get through this.'
- 'The more I strive for better sleep, the worse my sleep will be, so I'm letting go. Enough sleep is not about the number of hours I've had.'
- 'The baby's crying really isn't doing harm and will pass by 16 weeks.'
- 'I have a loving partner, I have a sister who cares about me, I'm lucky to have 6 months' paid maternity leave, and when I was working I longed to be able to spend days at home like this!'

These psychological approaches try to get rid of upset stories and feelings by disputing them or replacing them, and if that works for you, great! But if you've already tried positive thinking and gratitude, yet still feel overwhelmed and out of control, this is quite normal. Life with a new baby teaches us that there are many things out of our control, not just the baby's waking and fussing. The human brain has evolved to be a problem-solving machine, so when it perceives a problem it will narrow its attention and whir away, throwing up all sorts of ideas about how to solve it, whether constructive or not. Very often, positive thinking and gratitude simply won't stop the brain churning out worry.

Fortunately, there are some powerful new techniques to help us when we are faced with the painful gap between what we had hoped life with the baby would be like and what it has turned out to be; when we are overwhelmed by persistent negative thoughts and feelings about our failure as a parent and how this will affect our baby. These skills come from a modern form of cognitive behavioural therapy (CBT) called Acceptance and Commitment Therapy (ACT), which is proving to be very effective for a whole range of mental health issues, including anxiety and depression. It turns some of the old ways of thinking about our mental health upside down.

ACT argues that mental health problems often arise, paradoxically, out of the frantic attempt to eliminate negative thoughts and feelings (either by internal struggle or by engaging in distractions and addictions). If we fight with our frightened and despairing thoughts and our miserable, exhausted feelings, the struggle itself consumes us. We panic because the baby is distressed, and then we *panic about our panicking*. We feel flat and unmotivated to interact with the baby or get out of the house because we haven't had enough sleep, and then we worry that we are experiencing the first signs of postnatal depression, the thought of which makes us feel even more miserable and anxious and despairing. It's the struggle itself that places us at psychological risk. It's the struggle that interferes with our capacity to go back to sleep easily once we've been woken. It's the anxiety about feeling so anxious that darkens the day and drains us of whatever energy we have left. Then, as we battle on, terribly afraid of what our thoughts and feelings might do to us, and desperately trying to get rid of them, we lose confidence that we can live any sort of meaningful life in the midst of the exhaustion and the baby's crying – we lose confidence that we can be good-enough mothers.

This is when it can be very useful to stop trying to eliminate or avoid upsetting thoughts and feelings, which are normal, and to change our *relationship* with them, so that they have much less influence over our life with our baby.

Karen: 'I've never been down like this before.'

When Karen goes to bed at night, dread sits like a black crow in her chest. When she drags herself up to start the day, the dreadful feeling is still there, bigger and blacker than ever, pecking, pecking inside her, and she wants to weep from desperation, she wants to hide under the doona and never crawl out again. But the baby is crying from the cot.

In between bedtime and getting up, Karen has had just a few hours' sleep. Her partner sleeps in the spare room, so that her tossing and turning doesn't keep him awake. He's doing all he can to help, but she only feels resentment because he gets to go to work while she's left to care for the baby. She feels panic that she's not coping; she feels guilt that she's damaging her baby psychologically; she feels terror because she's falling apart; she is certain she's a failure. Every cell of her body longs for sleep but she hasn't had a good night's sleep since the baby was born 3 months ago. She fears for her sanity.

In that first week the baby started to scream, and didn't stop for a month. Even now, the baby is constantly fretting and grizzling, and most of the time Karen is too numb or panicked to enjoy the times when he isn't. Often she feels as if she is floating above her body, in a thick haze of exhaustion.

'Do you have a history of depression at all?' I ask gently.

'No. I've never been down like this before. I've been a lawyer for 10 years, and I love my work. I'm good at it! Last year they asked me to be an associate in the firm and they've given me 6 months' maternity leave. I've got lots of friends. I know you won't believe it, but I've *never* felt anything like this!!'

'I believe it, that's for sure,' I say quietly. 'Having a baby is hard enough. But it's difficult to know what it's like to have a very *unsettled* baby unless you've been through it. Is there any family history of mental illness?'

'Not that I know of.'

The baby begins to grizzle. She reaches over automatically, grabs the handle, and begins to rock the pram.

'Tell me more about your sleep.'

'Oh my God!' she says, fighting back the tears. 'He wakes me, and then I can't get back to sleep. I lie awake for hours. I go to bed when he goes to bed, but I'm lucky to get 4 hours' sleep a night. I just can't go on!'

'No, it can't go on like this,' I say seriously. I take a breath. 'Karen, do you mind me asking, have you had thoughts of harming yourself?'

She nods grimly.

'Thoughts of harming the baby?'

She gives another barely perceptible nod, and the tears trickle down her cheeks. The baby continues to fret and she continues to rock the pram.

I look at her with compassion. Of course, this is the way the human brain works. It's designed to throw out ideas about how to solve the problem, how to get rid of the causes. As bizarre as it seems, that's all the brain is trying to do by bringing up these drastic and terrifying thoughts. And I understand how these frightening thoughts about harming the baby, in particular, which are so natural and common in situations like this, seem so monstrous to women, and grow bigger and bigger by the minute as they try to stuff them away in shock. The more they struggle with the thought, the bigger the thought becomes. It's like telling yourself: *'Do not think of a monkey.'* And you instantly think of a monkey.

'Do you ever leave the baby in a safe place to cry if you're feeling overwhelmed?'

She nods again.

'That's a really sensible thing to do. It gives you time to take a breath and settle yourself down.'

She is still nodding, convulsed by silent grief and shame.

'Okay. We are going to get you the help you need. We'll work on a whole range of strategies together, as a team ...'

'I feel like I'm so depressed that I'm harming my baby psychologically,' she blurts out with a sob, and begins to weep in earnest, with a heartrending despair. I place my hand gently on her arm, and wait. After a few minutes, I speak again.

'You know, you're doing a wonderful job taking care of him. I can tell that you're already good at taking all sorts of actions day by day to protect your baby from your distressed feelings – including reaching out for help today! We'll show you some other simple strategies to help with this, too. What really matters is how you *behave* with your baby, the actions you take.'

'Do I need medication?' she asks me through the tears, reaching for more tissues.

'We'll certainly talk about that. Postnatal depression is debilitating, but it's treatable – and I definitely don't just mean by medications.'

I suggest that Karen might benefit from a few days of residential support in a parenting centre. Soon, I am on the phone to my favourite perinatal psychiatrist, developing a plan between the three of us. In my heart, I believe that if Karen had received a different kind of help early on, which better identified and managed possible underlying causes of the baby's crying, and which also gave her skills for managing the distressed thoughts and feelings that inevitably arise, her depression might have been prevented.

BEING THE KIND OF PARENT YOU WANT TO BE

The best way to change our relationship with distressed and anxious thoughts and feelings is to practise a set of skills called mindfulness. But before we can develop effective mindfulness, we need to have thought about the kind of parent we want to be. That is, it's important to know what your parenting values are. Then, even when the baby is screaming and fretting and you are utterly exhausted, even when you feel awful and upset, even when you don't feel much at all for the baby, the skills of mindfulness empower you to act according to your parenting values.

Values are different to goals, because goals can be achieved (or not achieved, as the case may be!). Values are like the four points of the compass, or the stars overhead: they can't ever be reached, but they tell us the direction in which we want to travel. Your values are unique to you, like the shape of your hand or the colour of your eyes, and no-one can judge you for them. When we live life according to our values, we tend to feel a deep sense of satisfaction and meaning – even though we face hard times, even though we have painful thoughts and feelings.

Anything worth doing will bring joy and reward sometimes, and pain and distress at other times. That's how life is. That's how life with a child is. So knowing how to act in alignment with our values when the going's tough is a vital life skill, and very helpful if your baby is unsettled. Parenting by your values is like using the stars to plot your course across the stormy seas of life with a new baby. You might not always be able to see the stars for the clouds at night, you might be blown off course regularly, but when you can identify your values, you are able to take your bearings and hoist your sails again.

If I could give you a gift, it would be this: that you are able to allow yourself an unrestrained delight in your baby. That you could allow the enjoyment of her to be an important value, despite everything else that is going on. That you find time to focus on the tiny pleasures of her sweet and milky breath, her sloppy little kisses, her soft skin, her nestling into you. That even when she is screaming you take care to caress her downy head or inhale her scent, that you place little kisses on her cheek, cuddle her tiny flailing body in your arms. That you notice how incredibly helpless and vulnerable she is, her tiny perfect toenails, her sea-anemone hands, and create every opportunity for small joys as best you can in the midst of it all. That you return to her gaze and her funny smiles and gurgles, over and over, in those wonderful moments when she *is* calm and alert. This is one time in your life when you can love extravagantly, physically, indulgently. All the evidence shows that it's incredibly good for both the baby and you, in the short- and long-term, if you are able to do this.

PRACTISING MINDFULNESS

To be mindful is to pay attention to and be curious about the moment in which you find yourself. Today many people are engaged in various mindfulness practices, often as a form of stress management. Research shows that to be most effective in helping us improve our mental health and quality of life, the practice of mindfulness involves three equally important steps:

- becoming aware of our unhelpful thoughts and feelings
- defusing from our unhelpful thoughts and feelings
- expanding our attention.

Becoming aware of our unhelpful thoughts and feelings
In stressful situations it's normal to find ourselves at the mercy of rampaging thoughts and feelings that do not help us create a meaningful and satisfying life but, to the contrary, drag us into a downward spiral of despair and misery. Becoming aware of them means standing back and 'watching' the memories and imaginings and stories which play through our head, 'watching' the emotions, urges and sensations that rise and fall through our body, without fighting them. We notice the thoughts ('Here comes the thought that I'm a failure, that I can't do it ...') and we pay attention without

panicking or trying to push them away ('This is a story that my mind is telling me right now'). Similarly, we notice the sensations in the body that accompany emotions, paying attention to where they are located, without panicking or trying to push them away ('I feel a tight whirring sensation in my chest and all the muscles of my neck and shoulders are tense and my stomach is clenched').

In the crying period, a story that plays endlessly through your mind might be true ('I am bone-tired') or it might be false ('My baby will be psychologically scarred by the crying'). Either way, it's not the veracity of the story that matters, it's whether or not the story helps you live a satisfying and meaningful life with your baby.

Defusing from our unhelpful thoughts and feelings

Awareness of what's happening in your mind and body is not enough to get you through, though. It's also vital that we know how to stop being pushed around by our unhelpful thoughts and feelings (including by the desire to be a perfect parent!). That is, we need to know how to *defuse from*, or to separate a little from, unhelpful thoughts and feelings. Once we learn the skill of defusion, we are better able to act in a way that is consistent with the kind of person or parent we want to be.

We live in a world that asks parents to detach repeatedly from their desire to respond to their baby's communications because of the belief that responding in certain situations makes life harder. In fact, our desire to respond to a baby's cues is biologically hardwired so that our hormones and nervous systems synchronise with the baby's as far as possible.

In other words, if you value getting in sync with your baby, then going with the desire to respond (which we often feel in our chest or heart) is *helpful*, even if responding doesn't necessarily settle the baby right there and then.

In a situation where you can't respond to your child – for example, if your baby is sick and you are by her side as the anaesthetist places a mask over her face in preparation for surgery – the powerful desire to respond to her cries and pick her up is legitimate and natural, but *unhelpful*. Since you value preserving your child's health above getting in sync in this situation, you defuse from the desire to respond in the way she wants, though you still stroke her and speak soothing words. I am recommending defusion as a technique that helps you manage your internal thoughts and feelings when they are not proving helpful to you, or when you find yourself all caught up in them.

The human brain is very good at problem-solving. We have evolved to narrow our attention to the crisis at hand, to focus hard on it, and to find a solution. Unfortunately, this hardwired narrowing of attention during a crisis is much less helpful when the crisis is ongoing, like an unsettled baby or disrupted night-time sleep. Narrowing our attention onto the problem in these more long-term situations actually interferes with our capacity to find creative solutions, to notice the many other satisfactions that surround us, and to live and parent in a way that aligns with our values.

So after we've become aware of our distressed thoughts and feelings, and recognise that it is quite normal to have them, we stop fighting them, and defuse from them. To defuse from them, we might imagine that our distressed thoughts are playing in the background like a radio in our head or traffic passing on the street. We might allow our distressed feelings to come and go like the weather in our bodies. If we have an unsettled baby it might feel as if a hurricane has permanently lodged itself inside us, but we accept that this emotional turmoil is a normal response, which we can live with for a time by practising the right techniques.

The simple act of deep breathing (exhaling all the air out of your lungs, inhaling deeply and holding at the top of the inhalation then letting all your muscles relax as you exhale) is a surprisingly powerful way of turning down your sympathetic nervous system and turning up your parasympathetic nervous system. More than that, deep breathing anchors us in our bodies, regardless of the feelings raging inside us. As we practise deep breathing, we might imagine that our breath is surrounding the painful feelings and permeating them and quietly making space around them. They may well not go away, but our breath makes the space for them, so that they simply sit there alongside the many other sensations available to us in that moment.

A METAPHOR TO ILLUSTRATE DEFUSION FROM UNHELPFUL THOUGHTS AND FEELINGS

There is a metaphor that is often used to illustrate 'fusion' with thoughts and feelings, and the effects of 'defusion'. Imagine that your hands are your distressed thoughts and feelings. Now place your palms over your eyes. Notice how difficult it is to pay attention to the things that matter to you in life when those upset thoughts and feelings are in the way! Can you see the things that give you pleasure? Can you see your values? Can you think creatively about solutions? Can you see what the baby is communicating? Then lay your hands back in your lap. What can you see? The distressed thoughts and feelings haven't gone away, they are still there. But they are no longer right in front of your eyes, obstructing your capacity to see and to respond to the things that matter.

Expanding our attention

Expanding our attention is a powerful way to help defuse from unhelpful thoughts and feelings. We expand our awareness by directing our attention to the many other things that are going on in the present moment (in addition to those thoughts and feelings and the baby's fretting or screaming).

When I was young and idealistic, long before I had babies, I used to carry around a book by a Jesuit priest who, as far back as the 1930s, predicted that humanity would one day use machines to create a nervous system which connects us all.

Now, like many of us, I spend my entire working day sitting in front of a computer, including when I'm in the clinic. I google many times a day, store my manuscripts and patients' records in a secure cloud, and enjoy Tom's volleyball games streamed live. I use Zoom most days for meetings, and also for reading to my youngest grandson in New York City. Even my elderly parents send me emails. Digital technology and electronic media extend our nervous systems and change the character of our humanness in ways that we have not yet begun to understand.

The downside to the miracle of the information age is that we spend more and more time in our heads. Technology – our smart phones, tablets and laptops – offers life up to us in only two dimensions of the senses: hearing and vision. In a world of digital miracles, our problem is less overstimulation of the mind, and more *under-stimulation of the body* and the other senses.

It's possible to pay a great deal of money for courses in mindfulness. How much cheaper and easier to make mindfulness your practice in mundane life with a baby, as you change the nappy, offer the feed, hang out the washing! To switch off the struggle switch and watch your emotions and thoughts ebb and flow, like stories that you notice without necessarily believing in them, like a radio playing in the background. To expand your attention to other pleasant feelings in your body, to the breeze on your face, the aroma of the coffee, the sound of that kookaburra or car passing by.

Baby-time (whether you are moving between paid work and home or not engaged in paid work right now) is a rare and precious opportunity to unplug, to ground yourself in sensation, to remember a corporeal intelligence, to return to the landscape of the body (even if the baby is crying). Baby-time won't last long. By the end of 16 weeks, the most intense first immersion in baby physicality is over; by the end of the first year, when the baby can move around and becomes a toddler, everything has changed.

We have only the briefest of opportunities in the span of our lives to come home to our bodies in quite this way, to immerse ourselves in physicality, to give the abstract realm of the brain a break. We can let this embodied attention to the new child become its own rare kind of physical joy, we can cultivate the pleasure of it, we can deliberately seek it out, we can revel in it whenever the opportunity opens up.

If you notice you don't feel much for the baby at all, remind yourself that is quite normal, too – feelings of love come and go like the weather in any relationship, and of course may be chased away for a time or take a long time to arrive in the face of exhaustion and endless screaming. It's your actions that matter, and you can choose to create as many opportunities as possible to enjoy physical connection and interactions with the baby, regardless of any numbness inside you, regardless of how tough the days are. It takes time, sometimes a long time, to build up any important relationship, the more so if the baby fusses and cries a lot, and you don't have to hurry feelings of love. Once we defuse from our unhelpful thoughts and feelings (not just the presence of distressed ones, but the worry about the absence of positive ones), we are freed to decide what action we might take. In relationships, including in our relationship with our child, we are the sum of the behaviours we choose.

When your baby cries, bravely practise mindfulness – noticing your thoughts and feelings as you do what you can, knowing this is not a catastrophe. Gently bring your attention back into the present moment, over and over. Expand your attention from those racing thoughts and painful feelings and your baby's distress, to notice the environment around you, the sound of a dog barking, your feet on the floor, the breeze coming in through the window, the car passing down the street. Offer soothing little sounds, half-remembered songs and lullabies, tender loving words. Notice your thoughts and feelings as you wait and hold, wait and hold, allowing a deep kindness to yourself.

GETTING OUT AND ABOUT

Instead of planning your day around a routine for the baby, be adventurous and build your days around your own needs, taking the baby along for the ride. Schedule lashings of pleasurable activities and relaxing social contact! This is your chance to network, make new friends, indulge in physical activity, and have fun.

A baby learns to fit in just fine, as long as you relax and casually attend to his cues throughout the day, allowing lots of delicious micro-moments in which to pay attention to him and enjoy him, as long as he is bathed in a rich and healthy sensory diet. Throw the covers off the pram and vigorously engage in activities that make *you* happy. Put him in the carrier, facing outwards so he can see as soon as he is ready for that. Don't worry about whether he is getting enough sleep – he'll take what sleep he needs, as long as you use feeds generously and provide him with rich sensory experiences – and try something new:

- go on a 'park crawl' to find the most beautiful parks and children's playgrounds in your home town (you'll need them next year!)
- join a playgroup
- take a yoga class for mothers with babies
- join in a tree planting or some other community activity
- visit the shops
- go to a mothers and babies session at the cinema
- make a foray into your previous paid work environment
- rekindle neglected friendships
- spend time gardening
- visit an art gallery or museum
- meet friends at a café.

When my babies were small, I walked and walked, alone with them, or with friends: it drenched us all in healing daylight, it was exercise for me, rich sensory nourishment for the children. What does it matter, I thought back then, if I walked half the day?

GOING BACK TO (PAID) WORK

Around half of Australian women go back to work in the first year of their baby's lives, usually to part-time work of 25 hours a week or less, and they patch together childcare using family and child-care services as best they can. (Under 12 months, it's best if your baby's carer is responsible for just one or at most two other little ones, is affectionate and responsive, and available to care for your baby over the next couple of years.)

Breastfeeding mothers planning a return to paid work in the first months of the baby's life often build their stores of expressed breast milk. They may also feel a need to prepare the baby by adapting her to the bottle, particularly if the days apart will be long. If your breastfeeding baby won't take the bottle, trust that she will not starve herself in the transition, even though her volume of intake may be less with the new carer for the first day or two. Asking the carer to squeeze a little plastic cup and tip the milk to her lips usually works just fine while she's adjusting.

Women may also feel that they need to prepare the baby by adapting him to sleep routines. Although it's true that the baby will need to adapt to a new carer and their different daily rhythms, I don't believe there is good reason to change your own relationship with the baby in order to prepare for that. If anything, it's even *more* important that you are able to enjoy pleasurable and relaxed days together with your baby before you both face the challenge of return to paid work. Let the baby adapt to the new carer's style when the time comes. Life is likely to be tumultuous for a little while, as you all adjust, and a gradual return to work makes the transition easier if you can do it. But disrupting your own relationship with the baby *prior* to returning to work by spacing out feeds, trying to teach self-settling, or weaning the baby, is unnecessary and disruptive for you both.

Chloe: 'I'm going back to full-time work soon.'

Chloe is a political journalist with untidy black hair, a ready laugh, lively eyes, and a 3-month-old daughter.

'I'm going back to full-time work soon, and the guilt has already set in,' she says. 'Other mothers are the worst – they are *so* judgemental.'

She tells me that there are lots of women in her playgroup who absolutely love being stay-at-home mothers, but that choice doesn't feel right for her.

'I can't do it. I believe my child needs to see me as a strong, working mother. But the *guilt* ...' she adds sadly.

She continues: 'They don't think they are being judgemental, they try to put it nicely. "Oh, you're not maternal," they say!'

I understand the wound she'd feel with comments like that. As if the desire to work full-time isn't consistent with a deep and powerful maternal love!

'I'm *still* reconciling my own choices about juggling children and work,' I muse. 'To my mind, there's no right path. There's only your path, and my path, and your friend's path, and every other woman's path, each one different.'

'I'm lucky,' Chloe says. 'Between my mother, my sister and my husband, we won't have to use childcare.'

'That is lucky!'

'She was unsettled, you know, though it's getting better now. There were times at my very lowest, Pam, when I seriously questioned why I'd had a child!'

While I converse with Chloe, her partner thinks that our discussion is going on without him. He talks to the baby, cradling her across his chest in his arms, looking into her eyes, murmuring to her. She smiles, which loosens the dummy, and since his arms are full of his lovely little daughter, he nudges the dummy back in with his nose. Her grey-blue eyes mirror his.

Chloe says, 'I've just got to get the baby into a routine before I go back.'

'Why?' I ask.

She looks at me for a moment, quite taken aback. 'So the baby is used to it.' She thought this was obvious.

I laugh warmly. 'I know this is very different to what you hear. But the most important thing you can do is to get the hormones working for you, so that you and your baby are in sync as much as possible when you are together. Babies are very smart. They learn and adapt. They quickly learn that what happens with Dad or at childcare or with whoever is different to what happens with you.' Her husband is listening now, and the baby reaches out to touch his face with a wobbly little arm, wanting his attention. 'Let them adapt to the new way of feeding or the new environment or the new way of doing things when the moment arrives. In the meantime, why not just enjoy the time you have together? Why not let it be easy?'

PRIORITISING RELAXATION OVER HOUSEWORK

When my babies were little, I ignored the housework a lot of the time, particularly once Tommy arrived and I already had a toddler to upend boxes of toys and pull saucepans out of cupboards and leave wet washers on the bathroom floor. Well, I tried to keep on top of it, of course. But I prioritised our happiness and often I preferred to lie down and rest or do something nice for myself if they were both asleep. Yes, our house was often a mess.

Then, as time passed and Tommy grew less dependent, I 'pivoted', as the psychologists say: there came a time when everyone was calmer, including me, if our environment was more ordered. So I responded flexibly to their changing developmental needs, altered my approach, and kept the house if not tidy, then tidier.

The way I see it, particularly in these early months, the house might be chaotic and the dinner uncooked (a salad and yesterday's leftovers will do); the toddler might be making playdough pies on the kitchen tiles – but you are calm enough of the time, and that's heroic. The fact is, of course, you're not really lazy or slothful, you're working around the clock, mothering according to your values as best you can, available for lots of interaction and enjoyment and physical contact, which means you are letting it be as easy as possible, for everyone's sake, which means you are having as much fun as you possibly can, for the sake of your children's neurodevelopment, which means there are other more mundane things that you can't always get done, like emptying the dishwasher. And even though the baby cries a lot, you muddle through and everyone emerges just fine, better than fine – much better, the research tells us, than if you used sheer force of determination to bow everyone and everything and the housework, too, to your will.

BEING KIND TO YOURSELF

Care of the baby, with the accompanying exhaustion, lack of sleep, and endless physicality of care, minute after minute, hour after hour, day after day, *is* a heroic performance. It takes wit, courage, and perspective. It takes a certain trust in the ancient biological intelligence encoded into our cells. It demands that we reconcile with our human frailty and unhappy thoughts and feelings, rather than denying them or berating ourselves for them.

We may find ourselves to be really very chubby, leaking lochia in the early days (which is the normal vaginal discharge after birth) or leaking milk, we may be miserable, sleep-deprived, and feeling negative about the baby. These are all characteristics of countless ordinary women after childbirth, and we are required to be very tender with ourselves in a world that bombards us with ideals of perfection. Let yourself be plump and leaky. Accept the hateful thoughts about the fat belly, or the too-big-butt, or the cellulite thighs ('Oh, here comes that same old "I'm ugly" story again'), knowing that regardless of your body shape, regardless of how secret we keep it, this story is shared with almost every other woman in our society. Remembering that your bodily changes are a sign of status, of serious authority: you, the new mother!

Anchor yourself in the present moment, breathe, expand your attention to the baby, the environment around you, the sensations inside your body, not fighting the unhelpful thoughts but not focussed on them either, paying attention to other things around you as well.

Try to do something deeply loving for yourself often,

even if tiny – a frangipani flower placed in a little dish on the kitchen bench, a warm deep bath with the baby, enjoying the sensations of your faithful, beautiful, hard-working body, which has just turned into two people.

Exercising and relaxing

There is now plenty of research to show that physical activity protects against depressed mood, and helps you sleep better at night. If you are exercising with the baby by your side, the rich sensory nourishment that comes with being out of the home helps to settle the baby, too. Apart from walking with prams, strollers or carriers – which is easy to organise and a good fall-back position each day – there are more structured ways of exercising with your baby. Some parents go for bike rides with their little ones in special trailers. Others go to mummy-and-me yoga or dance classes for mothers and babies. Some take to the footpaths with jogging strollers.

Exercise is another opportunity to bring your attention back into your body so that you become aware of your body's alignment, and sensations and breathing. After exertion, consciously release any muscle tension, for example, that build-up of tightness in your shoulders, or maybe the clenching of your jaw. A few moments of deep and progressive muscular relaxation as often as possible during the day habituates a turned-down sympathetic nervous system, which makes it easier to slide in and out of sleep at night.

At bedtime, notice any tension in your muscles and release it in every part of your body as you lie down, so that you fall, fall, fall down through the mattress into the sea of sleep.

Keeping your relationship with your partner healthy

A new baby is a time of immense new challenge in your relationship with your partner (if you are fortunate enough to have one). Your relationship deserves care and thoughtful time investment, in the midst of all that is going on. If you have an unsettled baby, teamwork is even more vital and yet, understandably, it is often in stressful times that teamwork breaks down. Have conversations about what your needs are as you face parenthood together, let the other know clearly how best to support you, what feels intrusive, what is helpful. If one partner, most often the mother, is spending long periods of time alone with the baby, then baby-free time when the other partner comes home is likely to be vital, as well as an understanding that there may be little time for housework. Discuss your values. One book I recommend for those who find challenges surfacing in their relationship during the extremely demanding life transition of the crying period is *ACT with love* by Dr Russ Harris.

A MOTHER AND BABY ARE A DYNAMIC SYSTEM

For the past six decades, health professionals have attempted to help new parents overcome worry and fatigue by encouraging them to 'get back in control' of the baby's feeds and sleep. Of course, it's very attractive to think that the complex messiness of life with a baby, let alone a crying baby, can be reduced to a set of rules. But when it comes to powers of nature, modern humans seem to be slow learners. Forcing our will upon a dynamic system (like a mother and her baby) can turn out badly in the end because complex systems stabilise themselves through countless feedback loops. These are disrupted in unpredictable ways by simplistic strategies that intervene in just one aspect, resulting in unexpected outcomes. If we do manage to exert some sense of order upon the biology of a baby's feeds and sleep through routines and the premature conditioning of behaviour, the changes are often not sustained over time, and may turn out to have some unpleasant, unexpected side-effects. All around the planet, we are learning to work sensitively with ecological systems, abandoning the old ways of dominance and mastery. Even in the corporate workplace a profound shift is underway, hastened by the COVID-19 pandemic, from an emphasis on rigid structure and tightly controlled schedules, to an emphasis on flexibility and psychological agility, because the research shows that these qualities are the keys to productivity and resilience. We need to find new ways that work flexibly with (rather than force against) our own and the baby's biology in early life.

A DIFFERENT VERSION OF TIME

Modern women reap the fruits of the workplace opportunities our grandmothers longed for and fought for. It's likely that each of you, as parents, have already spent years in paid work in a world that values productivity, efficiency, achievement and success. You know how to delay gratification to achieve your goals. You know how to function within the metronome version of time: productivity maximised, schedules adhered to, punctuality a priority, days micro-managed, hours commodified.

But time with your baby, whether you are engaged in paid work as well or not, is a time of not *producing* much (other than perhaps some breast milk and the miracle of a baby who satisfactorily wees, poos and grows). It's important that both partners understand that this mental shift of gears is in the baby's best interests.

On another level, baby-time can be a time of enormous renewal and creativity, a time in which you hit the 'reset button', a kind of personal dreamtime into which you dip whenever you are caring for your little one. The metronome version of time disappears for a while, and stretched, flexible time plays out around you. The hours repeat themselves in spirals and circles, in slow ebbs and flows. It's a version of time that is available to you when you spend time with the baby, so that the baby becomes an emissary from another world, a little wailing angel who reminds you that there is another way of living life: here, now, in the body, in all the body's sweet joy and heartache.

Sleep is susceptible to rhythm. It's like waves on the beach. If we set up the conditions for sleep in a way that aligns with our biology, if we can notice our desperate, anxious thoughts and expand our attention, if we live our days habituating a deep and physical relaxedness as far as possible, then sleep will come at night. Sleep is not something we do. Sleep is a mystery that takes us, that comes for us, that draws us under, both parent and baby. While there is no such thing as perfect sleep, and certainly broken sleep is to be expected, we can remove the obstacles that get in the way of an easy relationship with our body's own nocturnal tides. Even when our babies are grown, some nights we'll sleep better, some nights we'll sleep worse, and the best thing is to expand our attention so that we take action to live a satisfying, meaningful day, even when we are tired.

Your own most resilient self is really just the self that gets by from moment to moment, not looking too far ahead and panicking, not thinking back and feeling bad about where you've 'failed'. Resilience is letting each moment open up to you in its mysterious newness. Letting the breathtaking abundance of life present herself to you, freshly made, over and over and over, this moment and this moment and this moment. Knowing that *you can do this*; knowing you'll be good enough and that, sometimes, you'll even be wonderful. It's normal to feel awful about the baby's crying, but it's what you *do* that matters – the pattern of your parenting over time, the little acts you take, hour after hour.

Mai: 'It will be alright.'

Ellie comes in to see me with her unsettled 10-week-old baby, her first child. Ellie is accompanied by Mai, her great-grandmother, who is wearing sensible sneakers, black trousers and a paisley cotton blouse that falls loosely over her tiny wizened frame. Mai is a patient of mine, frail now, her hair thin, white and cropped, but her mind is as sharp as a tack. And since the baby arrived, Mai spends two days a week at

Ellie's place, humbly offering up her company, helping out in little ways as best she can.

'He screams night and day,' Ellie explains. The baby is asleep in the big black padded pram. She looks at Mai, who holds Ellie's gaze for a long moment, nodding, then turns in her chair to face me. Mai is impossibly old. She was born in a dirt-poor village in Vietnam 94 years ago.

'He does cry a lot,' Mai says carefully, still nodding. Her English is good. She worked as an interpreter for many years. 'But other times he is happy. He smiles at me. He's a good boy!' She looks encouragingly at Ellie. 'It will be alright,' she says.

I take a history from Ellie, and Mai listens intently, lips pursed, a furrow of concentration between her brows. Her face is a network of crevices and lines, her papery old skin textured and creased over high cheek bones and hollowed cheeks. Ellie and I begin to make sense of what has been happening, and the old woman gazes on steadily, patiently, without judgement, eyes dark and intelligent. Mai lived through the terrible wars, her people were persecuted, her husband and three of her children killed before she could escape with the youngest two. She brings the full force of her spirit to this moment, determined as long as she has breath in her body to support her precious great-granddaughter and miraculous great-great-grandson.

'I tell Ellie, every day, that this will pass very quickly,' the old lady says firmly. 'Soon he will be a grown man with a good job and a wife!'

'What if he's gay?' Ellie mutters under her breath, annoyed, but then she laughs.

Mai's face crinkles into a wonderful gap-toothed smile at the sound of her great-granddaughter's laughter. So the baby cries, her ancient eyes say. But he also feeds and sleeps and grows. Yes, our busy minds and our fragile human hearts pound with thoughts and feelings the way the restless waves pound upon the shore. Let them ebb and flow.

There is in each of us a part that witnesses, that never judges, that can never be hurt. This part of us sees everything – our pain, our heartache, our restless frightened thoughts, our exhaustion, our joy, our fear, our longing to give our child the best of all possible lives. This part of us knows that there is, after all, only one way to make new life. One tiny step, and the next, and the next, moment after moment, day after day, inhaling, exhaling, being the parent you want to be, even when your baby cries, even when your baby wakes you in the night. Knowing you'll never be perfect. Knowing you'll always be good enough.

Appendix 1

An intimate history of mother–baby care in the English-speaking world

Knowing a little history is important if we are to understand why so much confusion and conflicting advice surrounds the problem of unsettled infant behaviour.

Once, I spent 3 days in England with a friend. We located two stone reliefs hidden in the Somerset countryside, high on the mossy walls of early Gothic churches. They were sheela-na-gigs, their crudely hewn, spread-open thighs and birthing vulvas celebrating new life, even as their hag's upper bodies and skeletal grimaces spoke of death. Around 1000 AD, when these reliefs were carved, early marriage was inevitable, and child-bearing relentless. In traditional cultures, back then (and still now), babies may not have cried much, but to be female was to know intimately, from girlhood, the mortal danger of childbirth. This is why the local midwife not only knew the behaviours which supported the synchrony of the mother and baby's nervous systems and hormones (that is, their neurohormonal synchrony) in birth and breastfeeding, she knew protective prayers, spells and rituals.

Sheela-na-gigs belong to these rituals of protection, and their location in the oldest surviving churches in the British Isles marks the transition from earlier folk religions to Christianity. In the thousand years since, the Virgin Mary of the Christian church has been the dominant artistic and written representation of the new mother in the West. Cultural representations are important, because they help determine how we feel about ourselves as new mothers, and what the permissible social behaviours might be.

Lively images of the Virgin did flourish between the 13th and 16th centuries as the old religions faded: the medieval Madonna could be plain, she could be tender or feisty, she could be distracted and playful, she could be plump and broad-thighed. She was even the exuberantly lactating Madonna, Our Lady of the Milk, who exposed her breast, dripping with milk, in pious nourishment of the Christ Child. Subsequently the Virgin Mary 'Mother most pure, Mother most chaste', became purified, sentimentalised, cerebralised. She became Our Lady of Sorrows.

Shockingly, the protestant iconoclasts hacked out the vulvas of the sheela-na-gigs and chiselled off the faces of the Virgins. Though the Madonna of the resurgent Counter-Reformation defied them, she was permitted only very narrow representations, her breast buried under layers of heavy blue cloth. By the time of the industrial revolution in England, my non-conformist forebears worshipped in front of bare altars, surrounded by empty walls, never a Madonna in sight, and this gap meant that cultural representations of the new mother were ready to be taken over by the new, secular, scientific stories of the medical men.

DR CADOGAN HELPS WITH CORSETS

When the industrial revolution took hold from the mid-1700s, rural livelihoods were ruined by the mass-production of machines and factories. Poverty drove peasant families into the towns and cities, where the male doctors and barber-surgeons began to remove the care of what they viewed as the unpredictable, leaky, dangerous, even catastrophic maternal body out of the hands of traditional, mostly untrained, female guardians. Respectable midwives, some with certificates from training programs in Europe, protested that the new metal forceps used by barber-surgeons did unnecessary damage. But the doctors offered exciting new technologies just as local and collective female authority was fragmenting.

In 1746, in that filthy, overcrowded metropolis of London, where half of all children died before 5 years of age, Dr William Cadogan wrote about the causes of infantile colic and infant death. He observed that the breastfed children of peasants in rural areas enjoyed better health than the upper classes, and he bravely aimed to make breastfeeding attractive to the upper class woman, despite the constraints of her delicate breeding and the complications of corsetry:

> It need be no Confinement to her, or Abridgment of her Time: Four times in four and twenty hours will be often enough to give it Suck ... It may be fed and dress'd by some handy, reasonable Servant ... whom likewise it may sleep with.

Unfortunately, Dr Cadogan had not sat with peasant families long enough to know the *patterns* of successful breastfeeding. From this time until today, well-intentioned experts advocate breastfeeding, but accidentally set it up to fail.

Soon, in the heaving new urban centres, most mothers had no choice anyway but to leave their babies in the care of older children or neighbours as they went to work on the factory floor, feeding them paps or gruels or, if they could afford it, cow's milk. Because of the curtailment of breastfeeding and the loss of its contraceptive effects, in both the aristocracy and amongst the poor, the gap between pregnancies dwindled and the number of pregnancies increased.

The doctors treated pregnancy as a medical condition, inspired by the modern French idea of the body as machine, offering ether during birth with the backup of the forceps (as well as leeches and blood-letting). Seeing a doctor conferred status on the woman who saw him, and their services were highly sought after in the cities. This great cultural shift had profoundly negative effects upon the social behaviours surrounding mothers and babies.

ELIZABETH DIES OF PUERPERAL MANIA ON TURRBAL COUNTRY

In 1849, just over the river from where my Brisbane home is now, Elizabeth Grimes stood on Turrbal country and signed her name in a fine slanting fountain-pen script, with a stray ink blot above the 's'. I pause for a long time before the microfiche of this petition, staring at the only trace of my step-great-great-great grandmother's life that remains. She was twenty-two, younger than my daughter is now, when she put her signature to this request to the Governor of New South Wales for land for a Presbyterian school. She'd married the draper from Warwickshire not so long after his first wife died, becoming stepmother to his seven young children, and he'd poured all his meagre capital, everything he had, into his re-constituted family's passage out on the *Chaseley*.

Elizabeth survived childbirth three times in what was a dirty, violent frontier town on the edge of the antipodean jungle. At the time of her first 'lying-in', there is no record of a midwife who held qualifications in the Moreton Bay district, and anyway, she and the draper would not have been able to afford a midwife, with nine mouths to feed. Back home in Warwickshire, women with children of their own who had an aptitude or interest made themselves available as midwives for a fee. But here, at the end of the earth, in a district of 1500 white settlers, the local ladies helped, and the doctor was called in with his ether, laudanum and forceps, if things went wrong.

Eight years after signing that petition, a world away from her mother and sisters, Elizabeth gave birth to a fourth child, and died. She died of puerperal mania, of 'insanity of pregnancy, parturition and lactation'. Her funeral procession, *The Moreton Bay Courier* reported, wound down by the banks of the Brisbane River to the Baptist Burial Ground, where the Suncorp Stadium is today. At the other end of that terrible summer, the baby died, too.

I tell you this story because puerperal mania was, you could say, an early widespread outcome of the breakdown in the social behaviours that supported neurohormonal synchrony between mothers and babies. It was endemic in England and the colonies, a broad, imprecise diagnosis that marked the frontiers of medical knowledge concerning mother–baby care. Doctors tried to prevent puerperal mania by advocating the use of chloroform and forceps during labour to shorten and relieve the pain, and by curtailing breastfeeding, to further limit a woman's exertions. Unfortunately, both strategies increased a woman's risk of puerperal mania, the first because of the devastation of unnecessary pelvic damage, the second because of increased numbers of pregnancies and increased risk of mastitis, breast abscess and septicaemia. This strange phenomenon of expert advice being directly contradicted some time later (known as a 'medical reversal') still persists in the care of mothers and babies during the crying period. Experts in different disciplines wear particular lenses with particular assumptions about causality, which affects the way they make sense of the matter. It's as if by giving birth we suddenly find ourselves in a topsy-turvy Wonderland with Alice.

My great-great-grandfather had lost both his own mother and Elizabeth, his stepmother, before he was out of his teens. He married the daughter of another immigrant and they had eleven children. Although the Queensland Lying-In Hospital was established 6 years after Elizabeth's death, within its timber walls unwashed hands spread infection, and death lurked in the corridors. For half a century only the most abjectly impoverished women used it. My great-great-grandmother and her respectable friends would have preferred the care of a Ladies Monthly Nurse – a woman who'd given birth to her own children and offered her services in the home or in small private lying-in facilities for 1 week prior and 3 weeks after birth.

Among my female forebears living in the Brisbane district in the second half of the 1800s, the stories are similar: they had seven, eleven and thirteen children; they regularly lost babies and young children, at least two deaths in each family; and the women died young, due to physical complications of birth or weakened by the exhaustion and poor nutrition of repeated reproduction.

In the final decade of the 1800s, when my nana was born into a poor protestant farming family in country Queensland, birth remained informal and domestic. Although there was also by this time a ready availability of foods promoted for infant feeding, mostly dried or condensed cow's milk, breastfeeding still worked in those days, thanks to the Ladies Monthly Nurses' surviving knowledge about the behaviours that supported synchrony between mother and baby, and the relative lack of medical technologies that interfered with hardwired mother–infant hormones. All but the most wealthy Australian women breastfed back then, but when my nana was born, female life expectancy was just 55 years; one in 200 mothers died due to birth complications; and one in ten infants died. Social visionaries longed to do something about this brutal waste of life.

THE BABY WHO NEVER CRIED

The campaign from the beginning of the 20th century to medicalise the care of mothers and babies changed everything for women. Today, the ravages of childbearing no longer define our lives. But this safety has come at a cost.

From 1912, in a legislative attempt to stop women dying in childbirth in Queensland, practitioners who wanted a licence to help birthing women had to be hospital-trained. With the Maternity Act a decade later, maternity hospitals sprang up throughout the state. In these hospitals, nurses trained in the Nightingale method, a health system innovation that was already saving countless lives due to infection control. The principles of cleanliness, order and routine; of measurement, nourishment and ventilation – so effective in the care of the sick – were now applied with similar good results to the growing numbers of women giving birth in the state-owned lying-in hospitals.

In 1919, my nana stood in her white cotton wedding dress gazing soberly out at her future, by the side of the seated, sun-bronzed farmer who was her bridegroom. Social philanthropists and doctors had just opened the first maternal and child welfare clinic in Queensland, and these soon spread throughout the state. Maternal and child welfare nurses were trained in the latest Nightingale methods and emphasised regularity, hygiene and efficiency as the new scientific approach to infant care and household management.

My father was a late baby, the youngest of Nana's four, born in 1933. By this time, standards of living were beginning to improve, and mothers were becoming consumers, at least in the cities. Women's magazines promoted artificial feeds (derived from a suitable brand of cow's milk) as scientifically advanced, and the maternal and child welfare nurses were formally trained in Dr Truby King's method of scientific mothering. His daughter, Mary Truby King, promoted his method in her highly influential book, *Mothercraft*. She contended that 4-hourly feeding allowed more sleep for mother and baby, reduced the risk of 'chapped nipples, abscesses, etc.' and aided digestion and appetite.

> Truby King babies are fed four-hourly from birth, with few exceptions, and they do not have any night feeds ... [the Truby King baby's] education begins from the very first week, good habits being established which remain all his life.

But spaced feeds, as we have seen, even if not as infrequent as the Truby King or Cadogan methods, make life harder for many women. Spacing feeds puts women at risk of mastitis and breast abscesses, and suppresses milk supply, which makes babies hungry, which means they cry.

By the end of World War II, two-thirds of Queensland births occurred in maternity hospitals. As the baby boom gathered pace, hospitals were plagued by severe staff shortages and overcrowding. Women pursued the goal of painless, scientific deliveries, and medicated labours (known as 'twilight sleep'), often combined with forceps, were common. Although most women initiated breastfeeding, medicated births and the Nightingale and Truby King rules seriously interfered with breasts' capacity to make milk. This is how our breastfeeding amnesia began.

By the time I was born, in 1960 in a country town in the Sunshine Coast hinterland, almost all births occurred in hospitals. After I was born, I'm told nurses wrapped me in a bunny rug and gave me to my mother to hold (though not to feed). Then I disappeared for hours, my mother says, while we were washed and tidied. The steepest decrease in breastfeeding occurred in those years around my birth, as commercially packaged artificial baby milk products became widely available, both compensating for, and contributing to, the calamity of the drying-up breasts.

The time of the first breastfeed was arbitrary in those days, anywhere between 4 and 48 hours after birth, and my mother was instructed in the first days to restrict feeds to a few minutes each side, gradually building up to a maximum of 10 minutes. She says I was produced from the central nursery like clockwork every 4 hours, day and night. My mother spent 7 days as an in-patient learning the rules of the hospital's breastfeeding management system. Although these scientific rules set many on a trajectory of breastfeeding failure, my mother and I were lucky: somehow, we adapted, and were among those who were able to continue breastfeeding.

Once home, Mum was expected to rely on the white-uniformed maternal and child welfare sister for mothering expertise. The local Methodist church, and her visits to that neat little weatherboard building owned by the Country Women's Association, were the mainstay of her early life with children. During the week, clinic visits were an opportunity to dress up and get out and meet other mothers. Every Thursday for the first 6 months of my life, and then every Monday for the first 6 months of my sister's life (she arrived just 1 year later), my mother sat patiently in the waiting room with the other women and their children.

Once called in, the clinic sister weighed and measured. She advised on infant feeding, 'settling techniques', and the introduction of solids at 6 weeks, starting with egg yolk. I was allowed 3-hourly breastfeeds for the first 2 or 3 weeks at home (which probably saved our breastfeeding), but from then on Mum had to go back to the strict 4-hourly routine. She could not pick me up between feeds, for fear of spoiling me. The maternal and child welfare clinic was the crucible, the examination: miraculously, my sister and I gained weight adequately, and Mum's competence was established.

I learnt the art of delayed gratification early on, and was classified as a placid baby. Not so my sister who screamed with 'colic', stopping only when the fourth hour came around and she was allowed the breast. Sometimes, Mum confesses, she would pick my sister up and feed her before time, because of her screaming.

'But you never cried, so I didn't pick you up early,' my mother explains.

I ask my father, 'Was it alright for *you* to cuddle me at feed-times too Dad? Could you give me cuddles?' Dad immediately grasps the significance of the question.

'I definitely did, love,' he replies firmly, over 80 now, hard of hearing but mentally sharp. 'I definitely did, at feed-times and when we went out.'

'Other ladies lived in fear of the clinic sister, and hated her,' my mother reports. 'But she was always nice to me.'

OUT OF SYNC

In my last year of school, second wave feminism reached Australian shores. Despite her pleas, my mother had been forced to leave school at the end of Year 10, but my parents expected my sisters and me to have careers like any boy. By the late 1980s, I'd qualified as a doctor, done a spell in Indigenous health, and opened my own little practice, where, in keeping with the times, some women liked to take the speculum out of my hand and self-insert for pap smears. Breastfeeding rates had picked up from the nadir of the '60s and early '70s, in large part due to the breastfeeding activism of Nursing Mothers of Australia.

When my daughter Emma was born in 1990, she was kept separate from me in a nursery at the Royal Brisbane Women's Hospital, but by the turn of the century, large central nurseries were disappearing. Because it's now known that separation in the sensitive first hours and days disrupts breastfeeding and bonding, most babies today receive skin-to-skin contact immediately after birth, and room in with their mothers. Birth itself, though, remains profoundly medicalised and technologised: one in three women giving birth in Australia will have a caesarean section, and about one in three will have epidurals. Midwives have little time on the wards to meet the needs of each new mother, who is usually sent home within a day or two of the birth. Breastfeeding durations, if anything, have again declined in recent years.

Medicalisation of mother–baby care is one of Homo sapiens most brilliant adaptations, protecting child-bearing women and their babies from the intimate horror of biological dissolution. But as doctors hurried to save our lives, infant care lost its moorings, and the social behaviours that support the neurohormonal synchrony between a mother and baby have been profoundly disrupted.

Technologised birth (with its accompanying medications

and possible mother–baby separation in the first hours afterwards) affects the baby's primitive neurological reflexes, and the mother's milk supply, which directly interfere with feeding. Feeding is intimately related to the baby's biological drives for sensory nourishment and sleep. Yet as a result of our history, health professionals are not yet adequately trained in the prevention, identification and repair of clinical problems that may arise in these areas between mothers and babies. Worse, many are trained to promote rules about how to read and respond to baby's communications, which families are supposed to apply if they want the best for their child (and who doesn't want the best for their child?) but which make unsettled behaviour worse. In other words, health professionals are not only inadequately trained to help remove clinical obstacles to mother–baby synchrony but are told to give advice and rules which interfere with the single most important mechanism that makes families adaptable and resilient, the capacity to be flexible and to experiment in communications with their unique baby.

As a result, life after birth is seriously out of sync for many families in the West. Like Alice, the keys they are given won't open any doors in the long, dark hall. Being 'out of sync' means that being with the baby doesn't feel particularly pleasant a lot of the time. Maybe the baby won't settle at the breast or bottle, fretting and fussing and back-arching when his mother tries to feed him. Maybe he wakes very frequently day and night, grizzles for hours, or screams. Parents find it hard to know what the baby needs and nothing seems to help. The nights are long and nightmarish. They feel ill with exhaustion. Worst of all, a mother often begins to experience herself as incompetent – she feels disempowered, she blames herself, she despairs. That most get through all of this without ill effects in the end is testimony to the remarkable resilience of families!

We are at the tail-end of a century-long revolution in mother–baby care. This one final important matter of supporting the neurohormonal synchrony of mothers and babies requires attention before we can say, in the West, that our brilliant transformation of child-bearing is complete.

APPENDIX 2

NEURODEVELOPMENTAL CHALLENGES AND THE CRYING BABY

In the West, at the same time as the incidence of physical health problems in children has been decreasing due to improvements in medical care, vaccinations, nutrition, hygiene and safety, the number of children diagnosed with neurodevelopmental disorders has increased dramatically. Neurodevelopmental disorders include autistic spectrum disorders, attention deficit hyperactivity disorder, and sensory processing disorder.

Children with an autistic spectrum disorder may have problems in communication and social interactions, and of imagination and memory, as well as impaired muscle coordination. Children with a sensory processing disorder are often referred to as 'out of sync' children, with 'poor sensory IQ', and show either a hyper- or hypo-responsiveness to sensory stimuli. A sensory processing disorder may or may not be part of an autistic spectrum disorder. Children with attention deficit hyperactivity disorder show difficulty sustaining attention, impulsiveness and learning difficulties.

These disorders are believed to result from faulty wiring of the brain in early life, emerging out of a complex interplay of genetic susceptibility, and social and environmental factors. The interaction of these factors is mediated by the epigenome. That is, genetically susceptible babies are more likely to develop a neurodevelopmental problem in response to environmental factors.

There are links between these three neurodevelopmental disorders and cry–fuss problems, particularly in the 5 per cent for whom the crying persists beyond the first 16 weeks. This doesn't mean that your unsettled baby is likely to develop a neurodevelopmental disorder. On the contrary, almost all crying babies have no long-term problems. But the fact that a very small number of crying babies are diagnosed with developmental disorders down the track gives me another reason to believe that any family with an unsettled baby deserves the best possible help as early as possible.

If we consider neurodevelopmental disorders through the lens of evolutionary medicine, pieces of the puzzle begin to fall into place. We know that infant care practices concerning feeds and sleep fundamentally shape the baby's early sensory experience. We know that a healthily enriched sensory environment in early life produces permanent positive changes in the physiology and anatomy of the mammalian brain (and these changes, it seems, may even be transmitted to future generations). That is, in the acutely sensitive crying period, neuronal pathways are being laid down in the cerebral cortex to form the neurological foundations for the rest of the child's life, in direct response to sensory input.

Yet for the historical reasons discussed in Appendix 1, Western babies often experience early unidentified feeding problems, which profoundly disrupt mother–baby synchrony at the very beginning of their relationship, during a period of exquisite neuroplasticity. Our babies often spend the first months of life in a relatively impoverished sensory environment to avoid 'overstimulation' and 'overtiredness', and parents are often advised to deliberately delay responses to their babies' communications, or to ignore the baby's signalled intent, many times a day.

Is it possible that a biologically susceptible baby who has not received enough healthy sensory stimulation in the crying period might develop a sensitised neuronal reaction, either positively or negatively, to certain sensory inputs? And that this goes on to affect the way the parents interact with that child? Moreover, evidence from babies older than 6 months shows that they can learn to shut down and stop signalling their hunger for sensation (for example, for physical contact) despite high cortisol levels. That is, some babies seem to cope with the stress of hunger for sensory nourishment by dissociating, or becoming hypo-aroused: the sympathetic nervous system turns up high, and the parasympathetic nervous system turns up even higher, as a coping mechanism, to shut down intolerable arousal levels. Perhaps it is the more resilient babies who scream and scream for sensory nourishment in situations of limited sensory input!

Is it possible, then, that a biologically susceptible baby, whose stress system has been reset by prolonged high levels of sympathetic nervous system arousal during the crying period is more likely to develop a persistent sensitised stress response, which goes on to interfere with the child's capacity to pay attention and learn in later childhood? What kinds of disruptions in the first hours and days and weeks might have a butterfly effect in the dynamic system of the family?

Today, as a result of the pioneering work of Dr Stanley Greenspan and Dr Stuart Shanker and others, the old belief that a child is taught to self-regulate through punishment and reward is being replaced by the understanding that a child learns to self-regulate as a consequence of being regulated by loving adults. We can help autistic spectrum disorders, attention deficit hyperactivity disorder and sensory processing disorder in young children by minimising stress, by 'scaffolding' the child's stress response with parental or teacher or therapist's support, and by stimulating (or appropriately regulating) healthy neuronal pathways through touch, proprioceptive activation, and movement. Before learning can start, treatment identifies and responds to the child's inner experience; calms down the child's aroused sympathetic nervous system through a range of caring responses, emotional and physical; and helps the child increase energy levels through physical activity if he has learnt to respond to stress by hypo-arousal (that is, by shutting down).

If we were to modify the strategies that are being applied to older children with neurodevelopmental challenges, and make them suitable for newborns and babies in the hope that we might prevent neurodevelopmental problems or compensate for innate low-level biological deficits from the first days of life, we'd end up with the approach I've recommended in this book, which is known as Neuroprotective Developmental Care (NDC or 'the Possums programs'. You can find out more at www.drpam.au or www.ndcinstitute.com.au). That is, we would help the baby's stress system remain set on low throughout the first sensitive 16 weeks as best we could, by supporting the mother and baby to enjoy a healthy satisfying feeding relationship from the very beginning, by helping the baby receive a rich and healthy sensory diet, and by encouraging parents to get in sync with their baby through patterns of responsive and reciprocal communications.

We will not always be able to help babies cry less, and my aim is to help parents enjoy their baby as much as possible, regardless. But there may also be neurodevelopmental reasons why as health professionals we need to do all that we can to prevent, and to offer early help for, cry-fuss problems.

SOME RESOURCES FOR PARENTS

Although there is a tsunami of information available for new parents, most of it filters the evidence through specific lenses, which is why there is so much conflict and confusion. Below is a selection of books and websites that may prove helpful. This list doesn't attempt to be representative or complete.

BOOKS

Coyne, Lisa, Murrell, Amy & Wilson, Kelly, *The Joy of Parenting: An Acceptance and Commitment Therapy guide to effective parenting in the early years*, New Harbinger Publications, Oakland, 2009.

Greenspan, Stanley, *Great Kids: Helping your baby and child develop the ten essential qualities for a healthy, happy life*, Da Capo Press, Boston, 2007.

Harris, Russ, *ACT with Love: Stop struggling, reconcile differences, and strengthen your relationship with Acceptance and Commitment Therapy*, New Harbinger Publications, Oakland, 2009.

Shanker, Stuart, *Self-Reg: How to help your child (and you) break the stress cycle and successfully engage with life*, Penguin, New York, 2017.

WEBSITES

Allergies
How to prevent food allergies
www.preventallergies.org.au/
This Australian website, also known as 'Nip allergies in the bub!' shares information about prevention of food allergies.

Baby's development
Developmental milestones
www.cdc.gov/ncbddd/actearly/milestones/index.html
What to look out for in your baby's development in the first months.

Social skills and mental health
www.self-reg.ca/parents/
This Canadian website by The Mehrit Centre offers rich resources about the concept of 'self-reg' for parents, including for parents with infants and small children.

Breastfeeding
Australian Breastfeeding Association
www.breastfeeding.asn.au/bf-info/general-breastfeeding-
information
Excellent information for breastfeeding mothers.

Possums Breastfeeding and Lactation
www.possumsbreastfeeding.com/
Comprehensive, evidence-based help for breastfeeding
and lactation problems which avoids overdiagnosis and
overtreatment of you and your baby, but offers effective
strategies for finding your way through.

Sleeping
Baby sleep info source (BASIS)
www.basisonline.org.uk/
This superb website by Professor Helen Ball and her team
at the Durham Infancy and Sleep Centre UK offers you
information about biologically normal sleep and sleep
safety, including a collection of photographs of parents
using the principles of safe bed-sharing.

The Possums Baby and Toddler Sleep Program
www.possumssleepprogram.com/
Comprehensive, evidence-based help for newborn (0–4 weeks),
baby (1–12 months) and toddler (1–3 years) sleep, including
how to protect your little one's motor development and
how to care for your own mental health and emotional
well-being.

Your emotional well-being

COPE: Providing support for the emotional challenges of becoming a parent

www.cope.org.au/

An Australian site which offers information and support through the perinatal period.

For health professionals

Dr Pamela Douglas offers masterclasses and accreditation in Neuroprotective Developmental Care at The NDC Institute www.ndcinstitute.com.au.

About Neuroprotective Developmental Care (NDC or 'The Possums programs')

The Discontented Little Baby Book details the Neuroprotective Developmental Care (NDC or Possums) approach to the unsettled baby in a way that is accessible for parents. You can read more at www.drpam.au or www.ndcinstitute.com.au. NDC rests on a rigorously developed theoretical foundation. It integrates the evidence across multiple disciplines to offer a clinical framework for the care of mothers and babies in the community, broadly suitable for application by doctors, child health nurses, midwives and allied health professionals. Because the unsettled baby is one of the most common presentations health professionals see in the baby's first year of life, building an evidence-base for management of the unsettled baby has been an effective way to build an evidence-base for clinical care that optimises parent–baby neurohormonal synchrony.

If you are a parent, you will be able to access The Possums Baby and Toddler Sleep Program (unabridged) and other parent programs at www.drpam.au. If you are a health professional, you will be able to participate in masterclasses and accreditation in Neuroprotective Developmental Care at www.ndcinstitute.com.au.

Publications which comprise the NDC evidence-base can be found at www.pameladouglas.com.au/articles.

ACKNOWLEDGEMENTS

I offer my heartfelt thanks to the two midwives of *The Discontented Little Baby Book*, my publisher, Alexandra Payne of UQP, who believed in this project from the very beginning, and my editor, Miriam Cannell, who has, with generosity and sensitivity, helped me present complex concepts in an accessible way.

I have borrowed the metaphor of 'the struggle switch' from Acceptance and Commitment Therapy educator Dr Russ Harris. I am grateful to Russ for his wonderful workshops and ACT resources! I have borrowed the metaphor of the guiding star from Dr Koa Whittingham.

Thank you to Jeanette Tyler for her valuable feedback on a draft of the book. I am also grateful to Louise O'Connor, Dr Andrea McGlade, and Professor Jeanine Young for critiquing relevant sections. I want to thank the health professionals and staff who have given generously of their time to support the NDC or Possums vision since we first started delivering clinical services in 2011. Your talent, support, and belief in this work has mattered deeply.

Maria Golding, Sophie Marsh, and the lovely women of the Brisbane NIA community have danced by my side from beginning to end, inspiring me daily. I could not have sustained the long hours at the computer required to both write this book and to continue the development of the NDC vision, without the pleasure of our shared fitness and mindfulness practice, and your encouragement.

Selected references

The Discontented Little Baby Book is not an academic work. Neuroprotective Developmental Care (NDC or 'the Possums programs') is detailed in more than 30 peer-reviewed publications, which are available at www.pameladouglas. com.au/articles. *The Discontented Little Baby Book* aims to make this information accessible for busy or exhausted parents. I include here an abbreviated list of references for each chapter.

PREFACE

Brownlee S, Chalkidou K, Doust J, et al., 'Evidence for overuse of medical services around the world', *The Lancet*, 2017; 390: 156–68.

Hoffman T, Del Mar C, 'Clinicians' expectations of the benefits and harms of treatments, screening, and tests: a systematic review', *JAMA Internal Medicine*, 2017; 177(3): 407–19.

Coon ER, Quinonez RA, Moyer VA, Schroeder AR, 'Overdiagnosis: how our compulsion for diagnosis may be harming children', *Pediatrics*, 2014; 134(5): 1013–23.

1: HOW MUCH CRYING IS NORMAL?

Douglas PS, Hill PS, Brodribb W, 'The unsettled baby: how complexity science helps', *Archives of Disease in Childhood*, 2011; 96(9): 793–7.

Douglas P, Miller Y, Bucetti A, et al., 'Preliminary evaluation of a primary care intervention for cry-fuss behaviours in the first three to four months of life ("The Possums Approach"): effects on cry-fuss behaviours and maternal mood', *Australian Journal of Primary Health*, 2015; 21: 38–45.

Wolke D, Bilgin A, Samara M, 'Systematic review and meta-analysis: fussing and crying durations and prevalence of colic in infants', *The Journal of Pediatrics*, 2017; 185: 55–61.

2: THE CRYING BABY'S NERVOUS SYSTEM

Douglas PS, Hill PS, 'A neurobiological model for cry-fuss problems in the first three to four months of life', *Medical Hypotheses*, 2013; 81(5): 816–22.

Hadders-Algra M, 'Early human brain development: starring the subplate', *Neuroscience and Biobehavioral Reviews*, 2018; 92: 276–90.

Mansfield AK, Cordova JV, 'A behavioral perspective on adult attachment style, intimacy, and relationship health', in D Woods, J Kanter (eds), *Understanding behavior disorders*, Oakland, Context Press, 2007; 389–416.

Shonkoff JP, Boyce WT, McEwen BS, 'Neuroscience, molecular biology, and the childhood roots of health disparities', *JAMA*, 2009; 301(21): 2252–9.

3: HUNGER PANGS

de Lauzon-Guillain B, Wijndaele K, Clark M, Acerini CL, Hughes IA, Dunger DB, et al., 'Breastfeeding and infant temperament at age three months', *PLoS One*, 2012; 7: e29326.

de Onis M, Onyango A, Borghi E, Siyam A, Blossner M, Lutter C, 'Worldwide implementation of the WHO Child Growth Standards', *Public Health Nutrition*, 2012; 15(9): 1603–10.

Howard C, Lanphear N, Lanphear B, Eberly S, Lawrence R, 'Parental responses to infant crying and colic: the effect on breastfeeding duration', *Breastfeeding Medicine*, 2006; 1(3): 146–55.

Huhtala V, Lehtonen L, Uvnas-Moberg K, Korvenranta H, 'Low plasma cholecystokinin levels in colicky infants', *Journal of Pediatric Gastroenterology and Nutrition*, 2003; 37: 42–6.

Odom E, Scanlon K, Perrine C, Grummer-Strawn L, 'Reasons for earlier than desired cessation of breastfeeding', *Pediatrics*, 2013; 131(3): e726–32.

Renfrew M, Pokhrel S, Quigley M, McCormick F, Fox-Rushby J, Dodds R, et al., *Preventing disease and saving resources: the potential contribution of increasing breastfeeding rates in the UK*, Unicef UK, London, 2012.

Thompson RE, Kildea SV, Marclay LM, Kruske S, 'An account of significant events influencing Australian breastfeeding practice over the last 40 years', *Women and Birth*, 2011; 24(3): 97–104.

4: TUMMY TROUBLES

Carnes D, Plunkett A, Ellwood J, et al., 'Manual therapy for unsettled, distressed and excessively crying infants: a systematic review and meta-analyses', *BMJ Open*, 2018; 8: e019040.

Castellani C, Singer G, Kashofer K, et al., 'The influence of proton pump inhibitors on the fecal microbiome of infants with gastroesophageal reflux – a prospective longitudinal interventional study', *Frontiers in Cellular Infection and Microbiology*, 2017; 7: 444.

Douglas P, 'The rise and fall of infant reflux', *Griffith Review*, 2011; 32: 241–54.

Douglas PS, 'Excessive crying and gastro-oesophageal reflux disease in infants: misalignment of biology and culture', *Medical Hypotheses*, 2005; 64(5): 887–98.

Douglas P, Hill P, 'Managing infants who cry excessively in the first few months of life', *BMJ*, 2011; 343: d7772.

Douglas PS, Hill PS, 'The crying baby: what approach?', *Current Opinion in Pediatrics*, 2011; 23(5): 523–9.

Dryl R, Szajewska H, 'Probiotics for management of infantile colic: a systematic review of randomized controlled trials', *Archives of Medical Science*, 2018; 14(5): 1137–43.

Dubois NE, Gregory KE, 'Characterizing the intestinal microbiome in infantile colic: findings based on an integrative review of the literature', *Biological Research for Nursing*, 2016; 18(3): 307–15.

Ellwood J, Draper-Rodi J, Carnes D, 'Comparison of common interventions for the treatment of infantile colic: a systematic review of reviews and guidelines', *BMJ Open*, 2020; 10: e035405.

Gieruszczak-Bialek D, Konarska Z, Skorka A, et al., 'No effect of proton pump inhibitors on crying and irritability in infants: systematic review of randomized controlled trials', *The Journal of Pediatrics*, 2015; 166(3): 767–70.

Gordon M, Biagioli E, Sorrenti M, et al., 'Dietary modifications for infantile colic', *Cochrane Database of Systematic Reviews*, 2018; 10(CD011029): doi: 10.1002/14651858.CD011029. pub2.

Hjern A, Lindblom K, Reuter A, et al., 'A systematic review of prevention and treatment of infantile colic', *Acta Paediatrica*, 2020; 109(9): 1733–44.

Ierodiakonou D, Garcia-Larsen V, Logan A, et al., 'Timing of allergenic food introduction to the infant diet and risk of allergic or autoimmune disease', *JAMA*, 2016; 316(11): doi: 10.1001/jaja.2016.12623.

Kuhn B, Young A, Justice AE, et al., 'Infant acid suppression use is associated with the development of eosinophilic esophagitis', *Diseases of the Esophagus*, 2020; 33(10): 1–4.

Malchodi L, 'Early acid suppression therapy exposure and fracture in young children', *Pediatrics*, 2019; 144: e20182625.

Mitre E, Susi A, Kropp LE, et al., 'Association between use of acid-suppressive medications and antibiotics during infancy and allergic diseases in early childhood', *JAMA Pediatrics*, 2018; 172(6): doi: 10.1001/jamapediatrics.2018.0315.

Munblit D, Perkin MR, Palmer D, et al., 'Assessment of evidence about common infant symptoms and cow's milk allergy', *JAMA Pediatrics*, 2020; 174(6): 599–608.

Pärtty A, Kalliomäki M, Salminen S, et al., 'Infantile colic is associated with low-grade systematic inflammation', *Journal of Pediatric Gastroenterology and Nutrition*, 2017; 64(5): 691–5.

Perry R, Leach V, Penfold C, et al., 'An overview of systematic reviews of complementary and alternative therapies for infantile colic', *Systematic Reviews*, 2019; 8: 271.

Rhoads JM, Collins J, Fatheree NY, et al., 'Infant colic represents gut inflammation and dysbiosis', *The Journal of Pediatrics*, 2018; 203; 55–61.

Simonson J, Haglund K, Weber E, et al., 'Probiotics for the management of infantile colic: a systematic review', *MCN: The American Journal of Maternal/Child Nursing*, 2021; 46(2): 88–96.

Skjeie H, Skonnord T, Fetveit A, Brekke M, 'Acupuncture for infantile colic: a blinding-validated, randomized controlled multicentre trial in general practice', *Scandinavian Journal of Primary Health Care*, 2013; 31(4): 190–6.

Wang Y-H, Wintzell V, Ludvigsson J, et al., 'Association between proton pump inhibitor use and risk of asthma in children', *JAMA Pediatrics*, 2021; 175(4): doi: 10.1001/jamapediatrics.2020.5710.

Warner BB, 'The contribution of the gut microbiome to neurodevelopment and neuropsychiatric disorders', *Pediatric Research*, 2018; 85(2): 216–24.

5: FOR THE LOVE OF MILK

Boss M, Saxby N, Pritchard D, et al., 'Interventions supporting medical practitioners in the provision of lactation care: a systematic review and narrative analysis', *Maternal and Child Nutrition*, 2021; 17(3): e13160.

Brown A, Rance J, Bennett P, 'Understanding the relationship between breastfeeding and postnatal depression: the role of pain and physical difficulties', *Journal of Advanced Nursing*,

2016; 72(2): 273–82.

Colson SD, Meek JH, Hawdon JM, 'Optimal positions for the release of primitive neonatal reflexes stimulating breastfeeding', *Early Human Development*, 2008; 84(7): 441–9.

Dias C, Figueiredo B, 'Breastfeeding and depression: a systematic review of the literature', *Journal of Affective Disorders*, 2015; 171: 142–54.

Douglas PS, 'Re-thinking "posterior" tongue-tie', *Breastfeeding Medicine*, 2013; 8(6): 1–4.

Douglas PS, 'Untangling the tongue-tie epidemic', *Medical Republic*, 2017; 1 September: http://medicalrepublic.com.au/untangling-tongue-tie-epidemic/10813.

Douglas PS, Cameron A, Cichero J, et al., 'Australian Collaboration for Infant Oral Research (ACIOR) Position Statement 1: Upper lip-tie, buccal ties, and the role of frenotomy in infants', *Australasian Dental Practice*, 2018; Jan/Feb: 144–46.

Douglas PS, Geddes DB, 'Practice-based interpretation of ultrasound studies leads the way to less pharmaceutical and surgical intervention for breastfeeding babies and more effective clinical support', *Midwifery*, 2018; 58: 145–55.

Douglas PS, Keogh R, 'Gestalt breastfeeding: helping mothers and infants optimise positional stability and intra-oral breast tissue volume for effective, pain-free milk transfer', *Journal of Human Lactation*, 2017; 33(3): 509–18.

Estrem HH, Pados BF, Park J, et al., 'Feeding problems in infancy and early childhood: evolutionary concept analysis', *Journal of Advanced Nursing*, 2017; 73(1): 56–70.

Gavine A, MacGillivray S, Renfew MJ, et al., 'Education and training of healthcare staff in the knowledge, attitudes and skills needed to work effectively with breastfeeding women: a systematic review', *International Breastfeeding Journal*, 2017; 12: https://doi.org/10.1186/s13006-016-0097-2.

Jaafar SH, Ho JJ, Jahanfar S, et al., 'Effect of restricted pacifier use in breastfeeding term infants for increasing duration of breastfeeding', *Cochrane Database of Systematic Reviews*, 2016; 8(CD007202): doi: 10.1002/14651858.CD007202.pub4.

Kapoor V, Douglas PS, Hill PS, et al., 'Frenotomy for tongue-tie in Australian children (2006–2016): an increasing problem', *MJA*, 2018; 208(2): 88–9.

Kent JC, Mitoulas LR, Cregan MD, et al., 'Volume and frequency of breastfeedings and fat content of breast milk throughout the day', *Pediatrics*, 2006; 117(3): e387–95.

LeForte Y, Evans A, Livingstone V, et al., 'Academy of Breastfeeding Medicine Position Statement on ankyloglossia in breastfeeding dyads', *Breastfeeding Medicine*, 2021; 16(4): 278–81.

Moore ER, Berman N, Anderson GC, et al., 'Early skin-to-skin contact for mothers and their healthy newborn infants', *Cochrane Database of Systematic Reviews*, 2016; 11(CD003519): doi: 10.1002/14651858.CD14003519.pub14651854.

Schafer R, Watson Genna C, 'Physiologic breastfeeding: a contemporary approach to breastfeeding initiation', *Journal of Midwifery and Women's Health*, 2015; 60(5): 546–53.

Svensson KE, Velandia M, Matthiesen A-ST, et al., 'Effects of mother–infant skin-to-skin contact on severe latch-on problems in older infants: a randomized trial', *International Breastfeeding Journal*, 2013; 8(1): 1.

Thompson RE, Kruske S, Barclay L, et al., 'Potential predictors of nipple trauma from an in-home breastfeeding programme: a cross-sectional study', *Women and Birth*, 2016; 29(4): 336–44.

Wood NK, Woods NF, Blackburn ST, et al., 'Interventions that enhance breastfeeding initiation, duration and exclusivity: a systematic review', *MCN: The American Journal of Maternal/ Child Nursing*, 2016; 41(5): 299–307.

6: NOURISHING THE SENSES

Baroni A, Castellanos FX, 'Emerging insights into the association between nature exposure and healthy neuronal development', *JAMA Network Open*, 2019; 2(12): e1917880.

Bennett C, Underdown A, Barlow J, 'Massage for promoting mental and physical health in typically developing infants under the age of six months', *Cochrane Database of Systematic Reviews*, 2013; 4(CD005038): doi: 10.1002/14651858. CD005038.pub3

Douglas P, Miller Y, Bucetti A, et al., 'Preliminary evaluation of a primary care intervention for cry-fuss behaviours in the first three to four months of life ("The Possums Approach"): effects on cry-fuss behaviours and maternal mood', *Australian Journal of Primary Health*, 2013; 21: 38–45.

Hadders-Algra M, 'Early human motor development: from variation to the ability to vary and adapt', *Neuroscience and Biobehavioral Reviews*, 2018; 90: 411–27.

Jaafar SH, Jahanfar S, Angolkar M, Ho JJ, 'Pacifier use versus no pacifier use in breastfeeding term infants for increasing duration of breastfeeding', *Cochrane Database of Systematic Reviews*, 2011; 3: doi: 007210.001002/14651858. CD14007202.pub14651852.

Lickliter R, 'The integrated development of sensory

organization', *Clinics in Perinatology*, 2011; 38(4): 591–603.

Nelson AM, 'Risks and benefits of swaddling healthy infants: an integrative review', *MCN: The American Journal of Maternal/ Child Nursing*, 2017; 42(4): 216–25.

Prevost P, Gleberzon B, Carleo B, et al., 'Manual therapy for the pediatric population: a systematic review', *BMC Complementary and Alternative Medicine*, 2019; 19(1): 60. doi: 10.1186/s12906-12019-12447-12902.

St James-Roberts I, Alvarez M, Csipke E, Abramsky T, Goodwin J, Sorgenfrei E, 'Infant crying and sleeping in London, Copenhagen and when parents adopt a "proximal" form of care', *Pediatrics*, 2006; 117(5): e1146–55.

7: A GOOD (ENOUGH) NIGHT'S SLEEP

Ball H, Douglas PS, Whittingham K, et al., 'The Possums Infant Sleep Program: parents' perspectives on a novel parent–infant sleep intervention in Australia', *Sleep Health*, 2018; 4(6): 519–26.

Ball H, Taylor CE, Thomas V, et al., 'Development and evaluation of "Sleep, Baby & You" – an approach to supporting parental well-being and responsive infant caregiving, *PLoS One*, 2020; 15(8): e0237240.

Barry ES, 'What is "normal" infant sleep? Why we still do not know', *Psychological Reports*, 2021; 124(2): 651–92.

Blunden S, Etherton H, Hauck Y, 'Resistance to cry intensive sleep intervention in young children: are we ignoring children's cries or parental concerns?', *Children*, 2016; 3(2): 8.

Davis AM, Kramer RS, 'Commentary: does "cry it out" really have no adverse effects on attachment? Reflections on Bilgin and Wolke (2020)', *The Journal of Child Psychology and Psychiatry*, 2021; doi: 10.111/jcpp.13390.

Douglas PS, 'The Possums Sleep Program: supporting easy, healthy parent–infant sleep', *International Journal of Birth and Parent Education*, 2018; 6(1): 13–16.

Douglas PS, Hill PS, 'Behavioural sleep interventions in the first six months of life do not improve outcomes for mothers or infants: a systematic review', *Journal of Developmental and Behavioral Pediatrics*, 2013; 34(7): 497–507.

Etherton H, Blunden S, Hauck Y, 'Discussion of extinction-based behavioral sleep interventions for young children and reasons why parents may find them difficult', *Journal of Clinical Sleep Medicine*, 2016; 12(11): 1535–43.

Fangupo L, Haszard JJ, Reynolds AN, et al., 'Do sleep interventions change sleep duration in children aged 0–5 years? A systematic review and meta-analysis of randomised controlled trials', *Sleep Medicine Reviews*, 2021; 59: 101498.

Gallaher KGH, Slyepchenko A, Frey BN, et al., 'The role of circadian rhythms in postpartum sleep and mood', *Sleep Medicine Clinics*, 2018; 13(3): 359–74.

Kempler L, Sharpe L, Miller CB, et al., 'Do psychosocial sleep interventions improve infant sleep or maternal mood in the postnatal period? A systematic review and meta-analysis of randomised controlled trials', *Sleep Medicine Reviews*, 2016; 29: 15–22.

Matricciani LA, Olds TS, Blunden SL, et al., 'Never enough sleep: a brief history of sleep recommendations for children', *Pediatrics*, 2012; 129(3): 548–56.

Mindell J, Lee C, 'Sleep, mood, and development in infants', *Infant Behavior and Development*, 2015; 41: 102–7.

Öztürk M, Boran P, Ersu R, et al., 'Possums-based parental education for infant sleep: cued care resulting in sustained breastfeeding', *European Journal of Pediatrics*, 2021; 180(6): 1769–76. doi: 10.1007/s00431-00021-03942-00432.

Paavonen JE, Saarenpää-Heikkilä O, Morales-Munoz I, et al., 'Normal sleep development in infants: findings from two large birth cohorts', *Sleep Medicine*, 2020; 69: 145–54.

Smith JP, Forrester RI, 'Association between breastfeeding and new mothers' sleep: a unique Australian time use study', *International Breastfeeding Journal*, 2021; 16(7): doi.org/10.1186/s13006-020-00347-z.

Whittingham K, Douglas PS, 'Optimizing parent–infant sleep from birth to 6 months: a new paradigm', *Infant Mental Health Journal*, 2014; 35(6): 614–23.

8: ENJOYING YOUR BABY

Britto PR, Lye SJ, Proulx K, et al., 'Nurturing care: promoting early childhood development', *The Lancet*, 2017; 389: 91–102.

DeJong H, Fox E, Stein A, 'Rumination and postnatal depression: a systematic review and a cognitive model', *Behavior Research and Therapy*, 2016; 82: 38–49.

Gloster AT, Walder N, Levin M, et al., 'The empirical status of Acceptance and Commitment Therapy: a review of meta-analyses', *Journal of Contextual Behavioral Science*, 2020; 18: 181–92.

Matas E, Bock J, Braun K, 'The impact of parent–infant interaction on epigenetic plasticity mediating synaptic adaptations in the infant brain', *Psychopathology*, 2016; 49(4): 201–10.

Monteiro F, Fonseca A, Pereira M, et al., 'What protects

at-risk postpartum women from developing depressive and anxiety symptoms? The role of acceptance-focused processes and self-compassion', *Journal of Affective Disorders*, 2019; 246: 522–9.

Feldman R, 'The neurobiology of mammalian parenting and the biosocial context of human caregiving', *Hormones and Behavior*, 2016; 77: 3–17.

Salari N, Khazaie H, Hosseinian-Far A, et al., 'The effect of Acceptance and Commitment Therapy on insomnia and sleep quality: a systematic review', *BMC Neurology*, 2020; 20: 300.

Whittingham K, Douglas PS, '"Possums": building contextual behavioural science into an innovative evidence-based approach to parenting support in early life', in: Kirkaldy B (ed.), *Psychotherapy in Parenthood and Beyond*, Turin, Italy: Edizioni Minerva Medica, 2016; 43–56.

APPENDIX 1

Cadogan W, *An essay upon nursing, and the management of children, from their birth to three years of age. By a Physician*, 2nd ed., J Roberts, London, 1748; 25.

Davies RA, *'She did what she could': childbirth and midwifery practice in Queensland 1859–1912*, PhD thesis, Queensland University of Technology, Coopers Plains, 2003.

Douglas P, 'Milkmother memoir', in J Dymond, N Willey (eds), *Motherhood memoirs: mothers creating/writing lives*, Demeter Press, Bradford, Ontario: 2013; 105–30.

Thorley V, 'Initiating breastfeeding in postwar Queensland', *Breastfeeding Review*, 2001; 9: 21–6.

Thorley V, 'Midwives, trainees and mothers: maternity hospital conditions in postwar Queensland', *Birth Issues*, 2001; 10: 101–6.

Thorley V, 'Printed advice on initiating and maintaining breastfeeding in the mid-20th-century Queensland', *Journal of Human Lactation*, 2003; 19: 77–89.

Truby King M, *Mothercraft*, Whitcombe and Tombs Ltd, Sydney, 1936; 5, 66.

APPENDIX 2

Bilgin A, Baumann N, Jaekel J, et al., 'Early crying, sleeping, and feeding problems and trajectories of attention problems from childhood to adulthood', *Child Development*, 2020; 91(1): e77–91.

Bilgin A, Wolke D, 'Infant crying problems and symptoms of sleeping problems predict attachment disorganization at 18 months', *Attachment and Human Development*, 2020; 22(4): 367–9. doi: 10.1080/14616734.14612019.

Breeman LD, Jaekel J, Baumann N, et al., 'Infant regulatory problems, parenting quality and childhood attention problems', *Early Human Development*, 2018; 124: 11–16.

Cook F, Conway LJ, Giallo R, et al., 'Infant sleep and child mental health: a longitudinal investigation', *Archives of Disease in Childhood*, 2020; 105(7): 655–60.

Cook F, Giallo R, Hiscock H, et al., 'Infant regulation and child mental health concerns: a longitudinal study', *Pediatrics*, 2019; 143(3): e20180977.

Douglas PS, 'Pre-emptive intervention for Autism Spectrum Disorder: theoretical foundations and clinical translation, *Frontiers in Integrative Neuroscience*, 2019; 13: 66. doi. org/10.3389/fnint.2019.00066.

Fields C, Glazebrook JF, 'Disrupted development and imbalanced function in the global neuronal workspace: a positive-feedback mechanism for the emergence of ASD in early infancy', *Cognitive Neurodynamics*, 2017; 11(1): 1–21.

Fogen A, King BJ, Shanker SG, *Human development in the twenty-first century: visionary ideas from systems scientists*, Cambridge University Press, New York, 2008.

Greenspan S, 'The Affect Diathesis Hypothesis: the role of emotions in the core deficit in autism and in the development of intelligence and social skills', *Journal of Developmental and Learning Disorders*, 2001; 5: 1–44.

Smarius LJCA, Strieder TG, Loomans EM, et al., 'Excessive infant crying doubles the risk of mood and behavioral problems at age 5: evidence for mediation by maternal characteristics', *European Child and Adolescent Psychiatry*, 2017; 26(3): 293–302.

Rask CU, Ørnbøl E, Olsen EM, Fink P, Skovgaard AM, 'Infant behaviours are predictive of functional somatic symptoms at ages 5–7 years: results from the Copenhagen Child Cohort CCC2000', *The Journal of Pediatrics*, 2013; 162(2): 335–42.

Santos I, Matijasevich A, Capilheira M, et al., 'Excessive crying at 3 months of age and behavioural problems at 4 years of age: a prospective cohort study', *Journal of Epidemiology and Community Health*, 2015; doi: 10.1136/jech-2014.

Valla L, Cvancarova M, Andenaes R, et al., 'Association between colic and sleep problems in infancy and subsequent development, emotional and behavioral problems: a longitudinal study', *BMC Pediatrics*, 2021; 21(23): doi.org/10.1186/s12887-12020-02483-1881.

Williams KE, Nicholson JM, Walker S, et al., 'Early childhood profiles of sleep problems and self-regulation predict later school adjustment', *British Journal of Educational Psychology*, 2016; 86(2): 331–50.

INDEX

endoscopy 37
enteric nervous system 21
epidurals 218
exercise and relaxation 200–1

feeding reflexes 64–8
'feed–play–sleep' cycle 156–8
feed spacing 29, 44, 215
feeds
force, use of 87–8
frequency 82–3, 85–7
paced 112, 120
sensory experience, as 113–4
sleepiness after 74–6
flatulence, copious 55–7
formula-feeding 16, 98, 105–6
bottle-feeding technique
98–9
hydrolysed formula 53–4
reasons for commencing 27–8,
72
sleep and 147–8
fruit juice 37–8

gastro-oesophageal reflux
disease (GORD) 37–9, 45,
50
crying, impact on gut 45–6
inaccurate diagnosis of 45,
49–50
Greenspan, Dr Stanley 224
Grimes, Elizabeth 210–2
gut 21
bacteria 22, 62–3
crying, impact of 45–6
immune organ, as 50
sensitivity to brain changes
21–2
gut bacteria 22, 62–3
Lactobacillus reuteri 62–3

hand expressing 84
Harris, Dr Russ 201
hormones
cholecystokinin, satiety 26, 75
oxytocin 15, 75, 98

hospital births, increase in 215
housework 197–8
hunger 25–6
cholecystokinin, satiety
hormone 26, 75
hyper-arousal 126, 224
hypo-arousal 126, 224
hypoplastic breast 30–3

Infacol 36

jaundice 83

lochia 199
Losec 40, 45, 47, 58, 86, 124
love for baby 192–3

manipulative therapists 132–4
massage 129
mastitis 82, 90–2
medicalisation
birth, of 217–20
mother–baby care 218
milk-drunk 75–6
mindfulness, practising 186–93
awareness of thoughts/feelings
186–7
defusing from unhelpful
thoughts and feelings
187–9
expanding attention 190–3
mother
see also depression
anxiety, postnatal 173–5
baby-time, different version of
time 202–4
biological interaction with
baby 15
brain neuroplasticity post-
birth 14–5
exercise and relaxation 200–1
flexibility, need for 203–4
housework 197–8
'out of sync' with baby 15–7
paid work, return to 194–7
relationship with partner 201